This Book
Belongs to

_____

_____

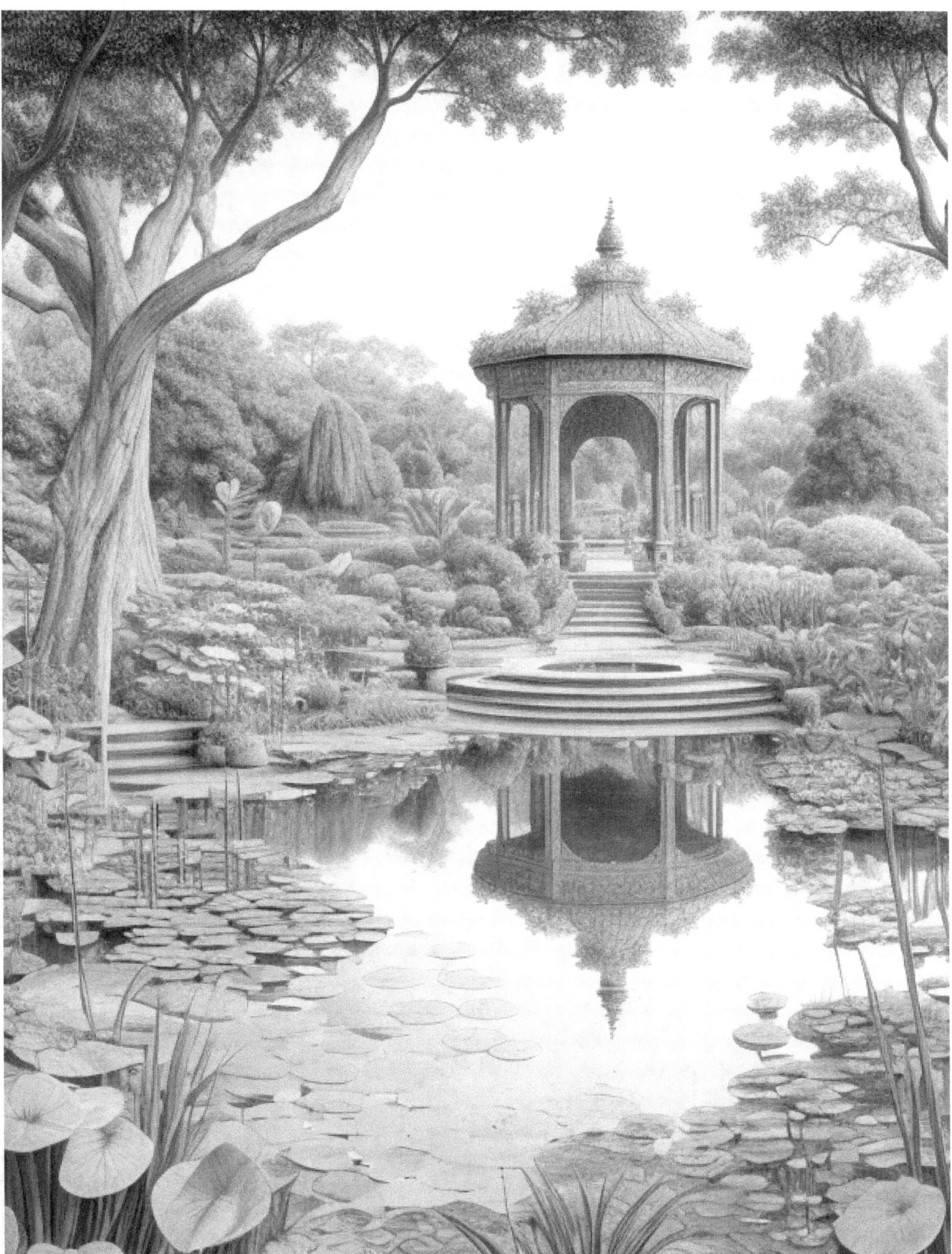

This Page is Intentionally Left Blank to Prevent Bleed Through.

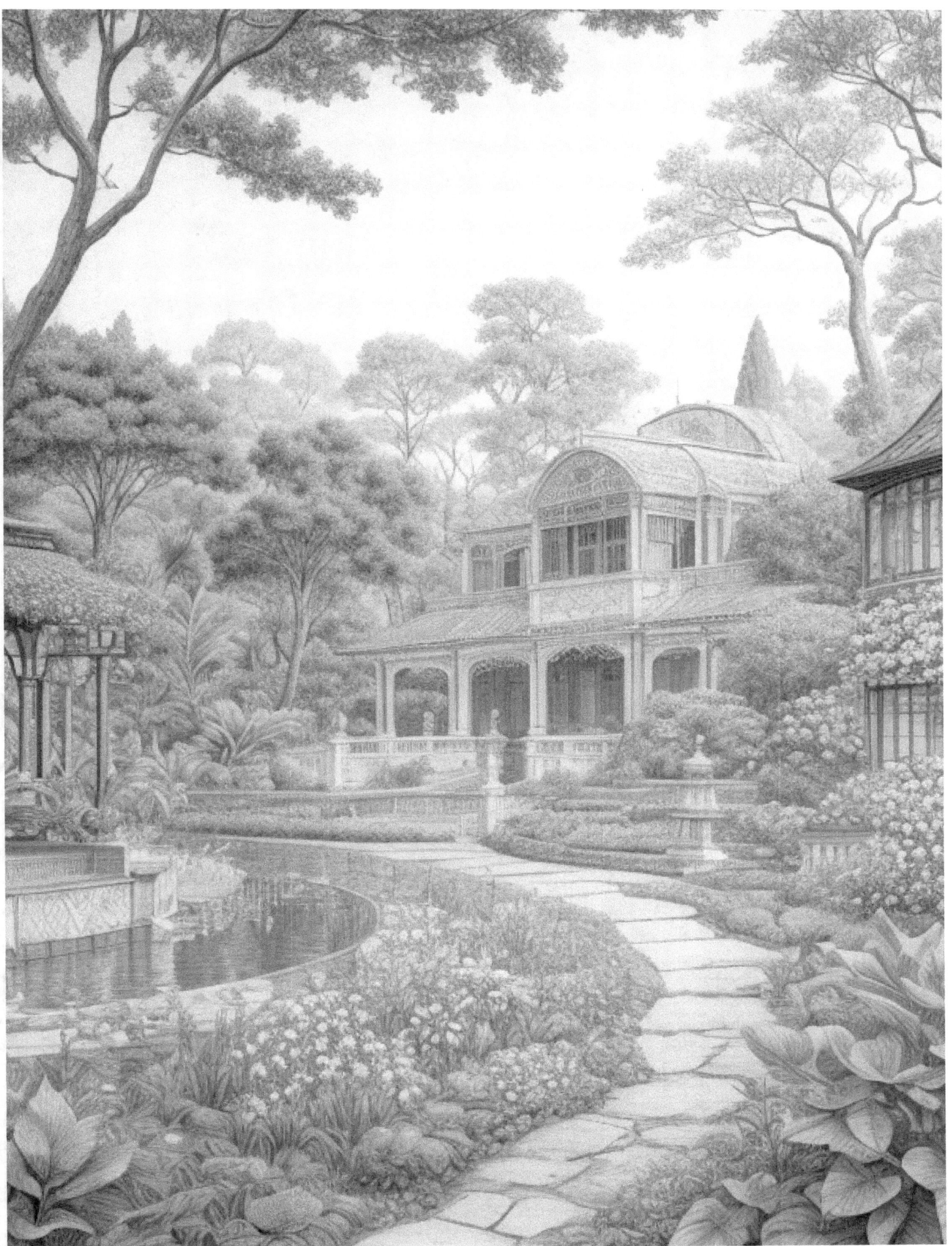

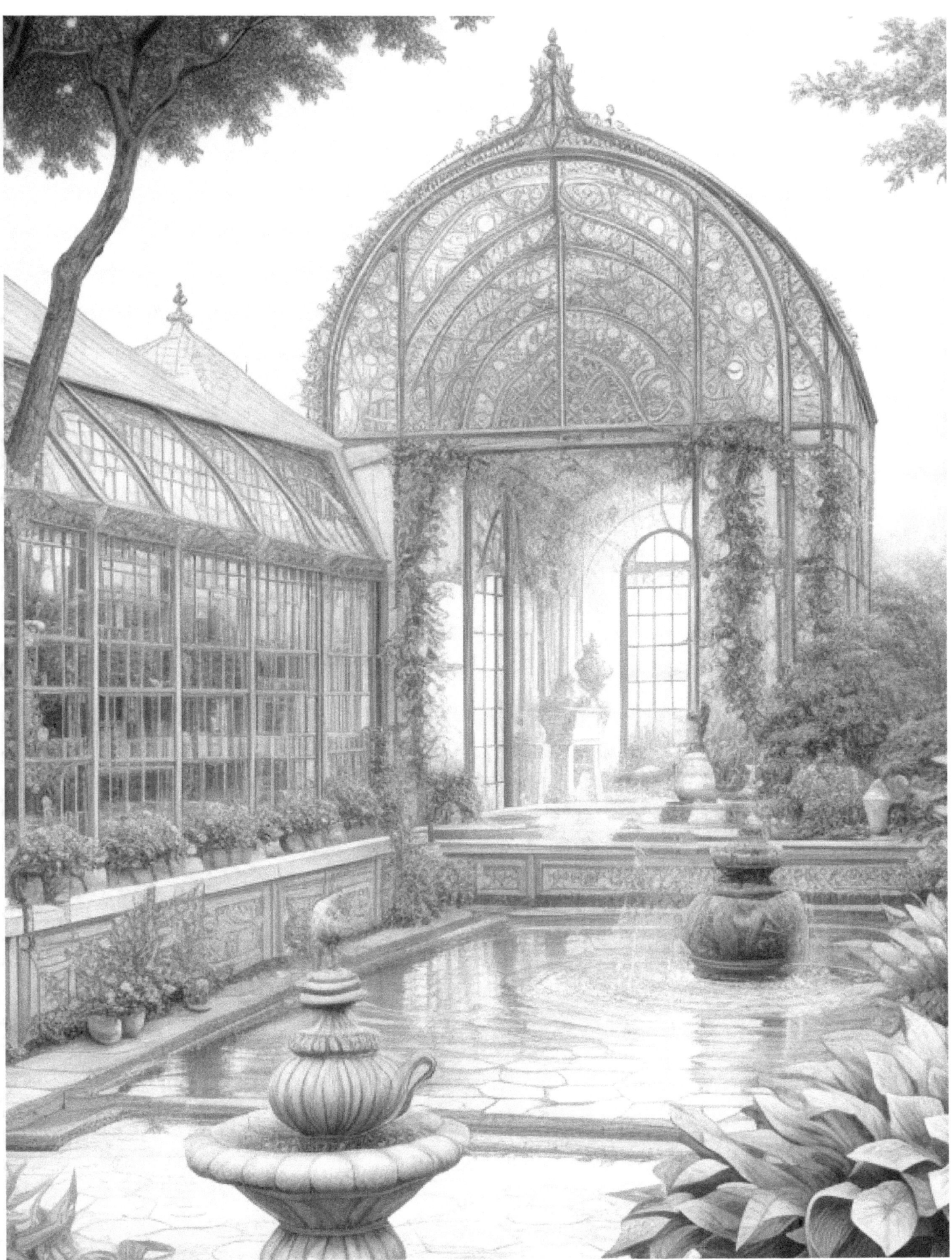

This Page is Intentionally Left Blank to Prevent Bleed Through.

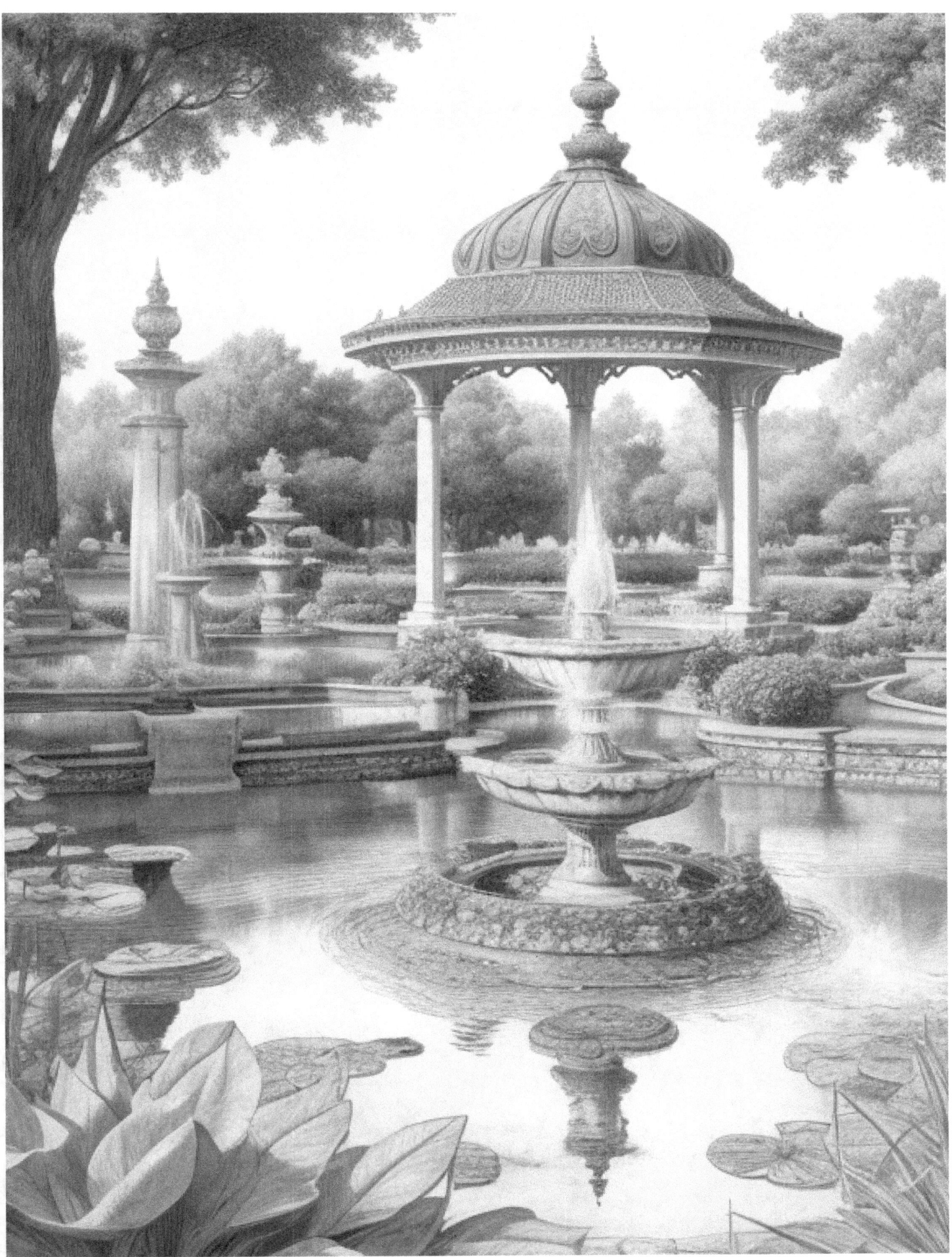

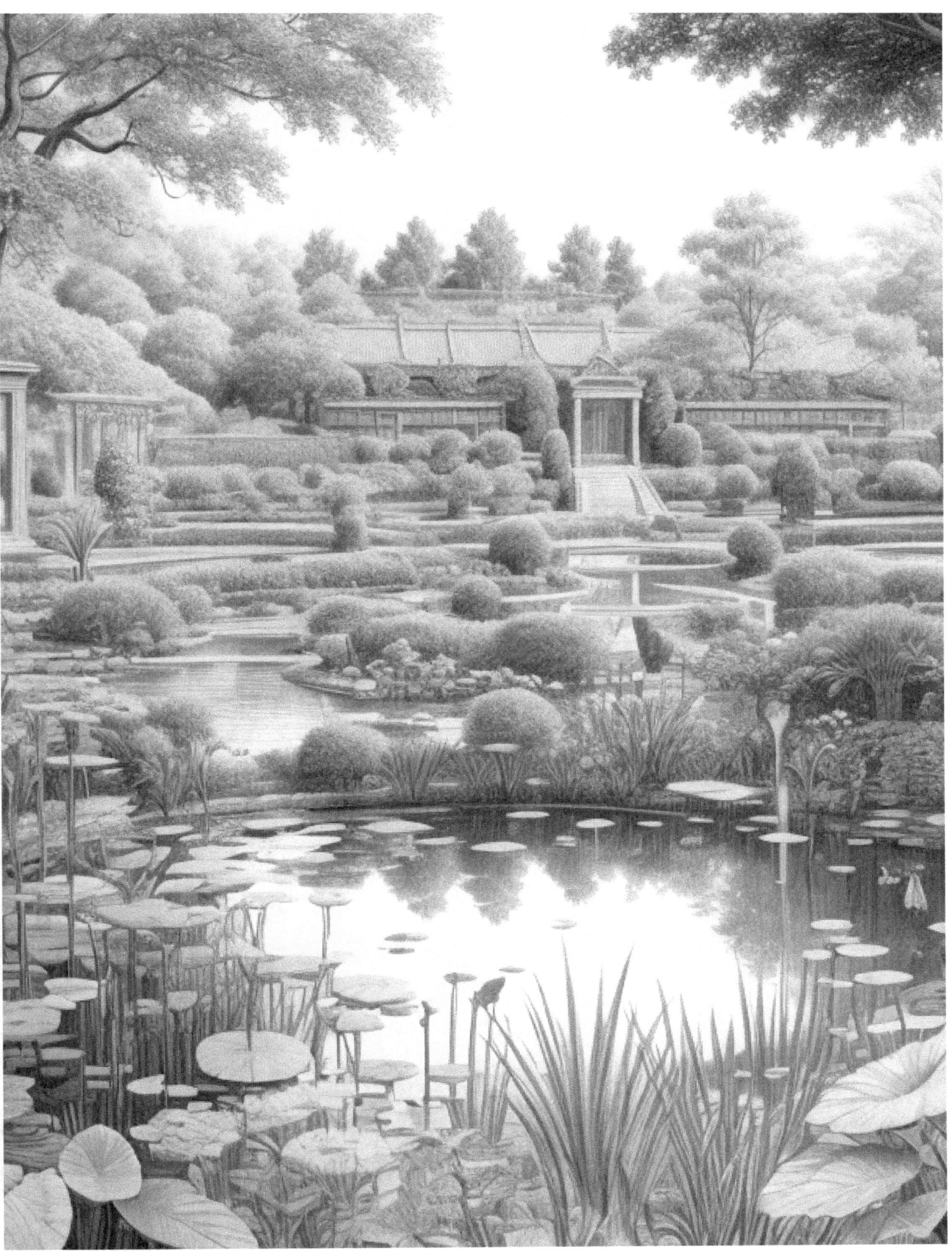

This Page is Intentionally Left Blank to Prevent Bleed Through.

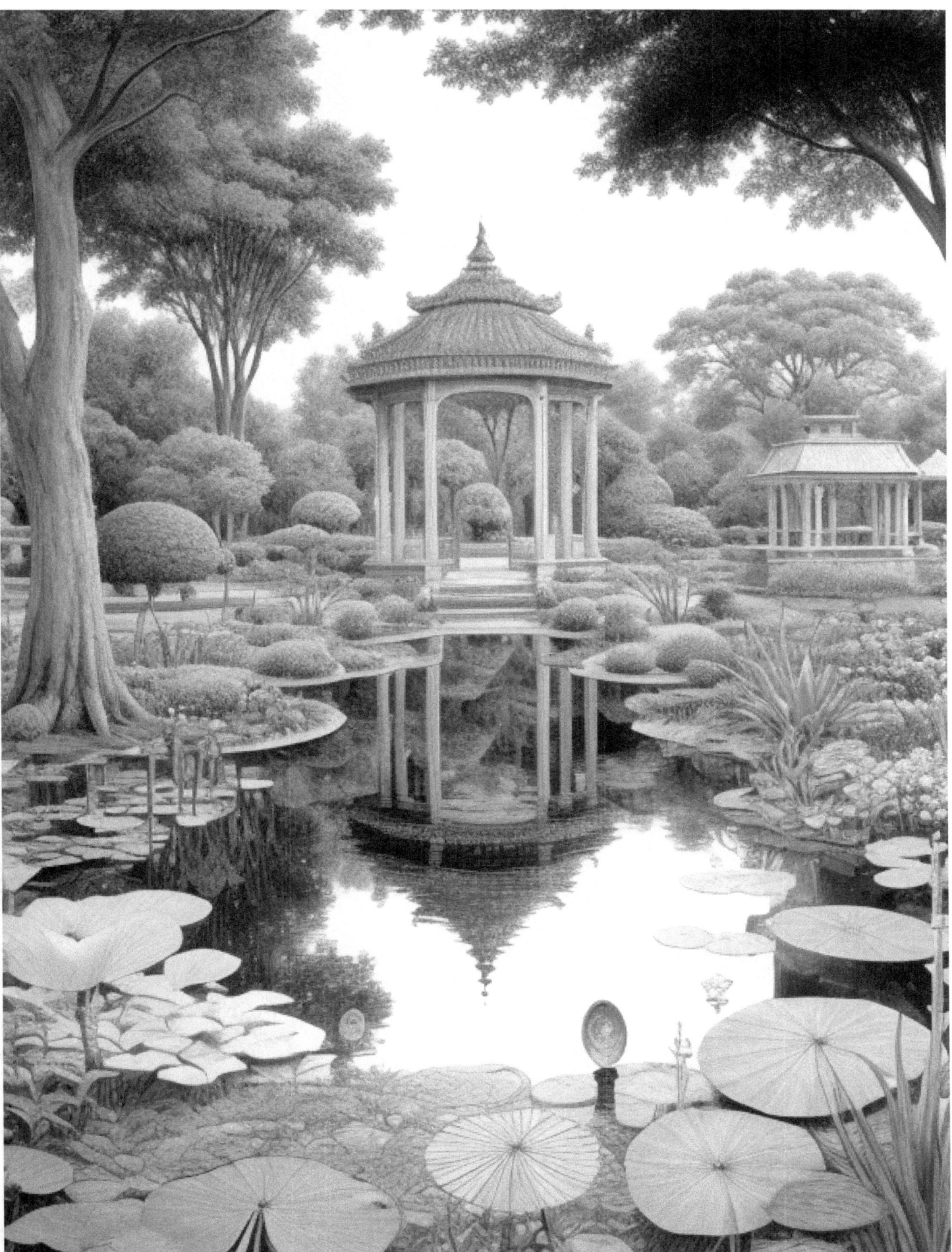

This Page is Intentionally Left Blank to Prevent Bleed Through.

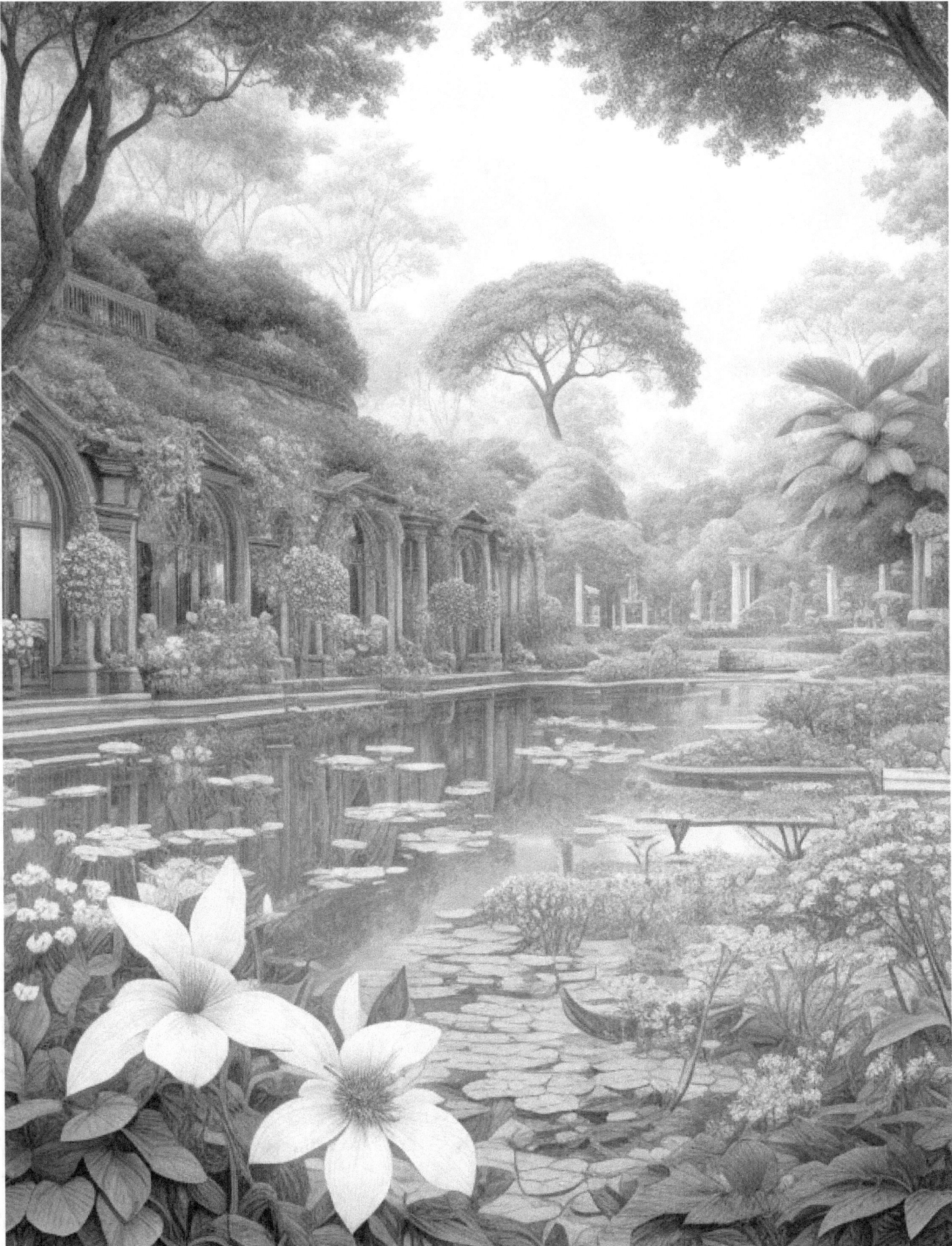

This Page is Intentionally Left Blank to Prevent Bleed Through.

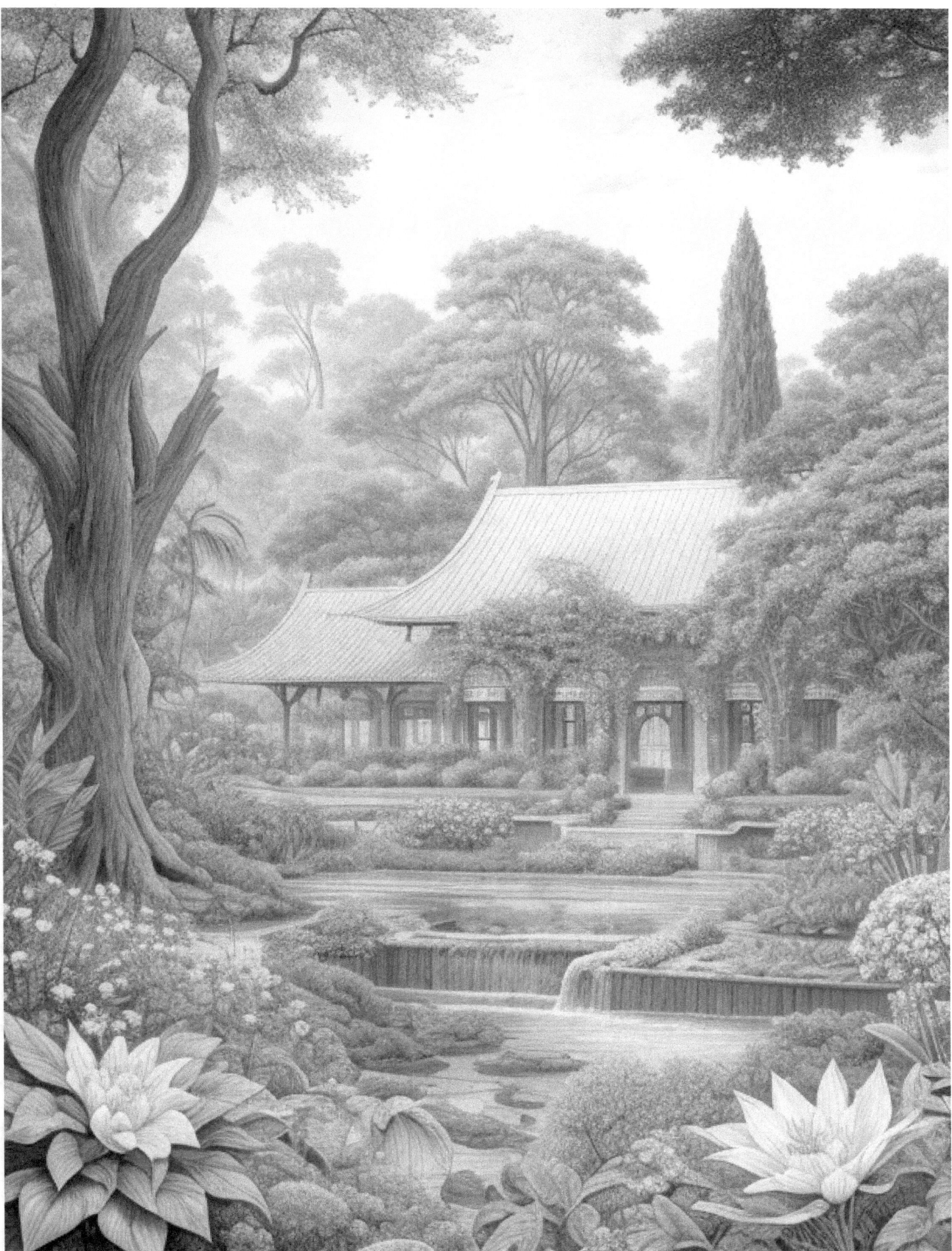

This Page is Intentionally Left Blank to Prevent Bleed Through.

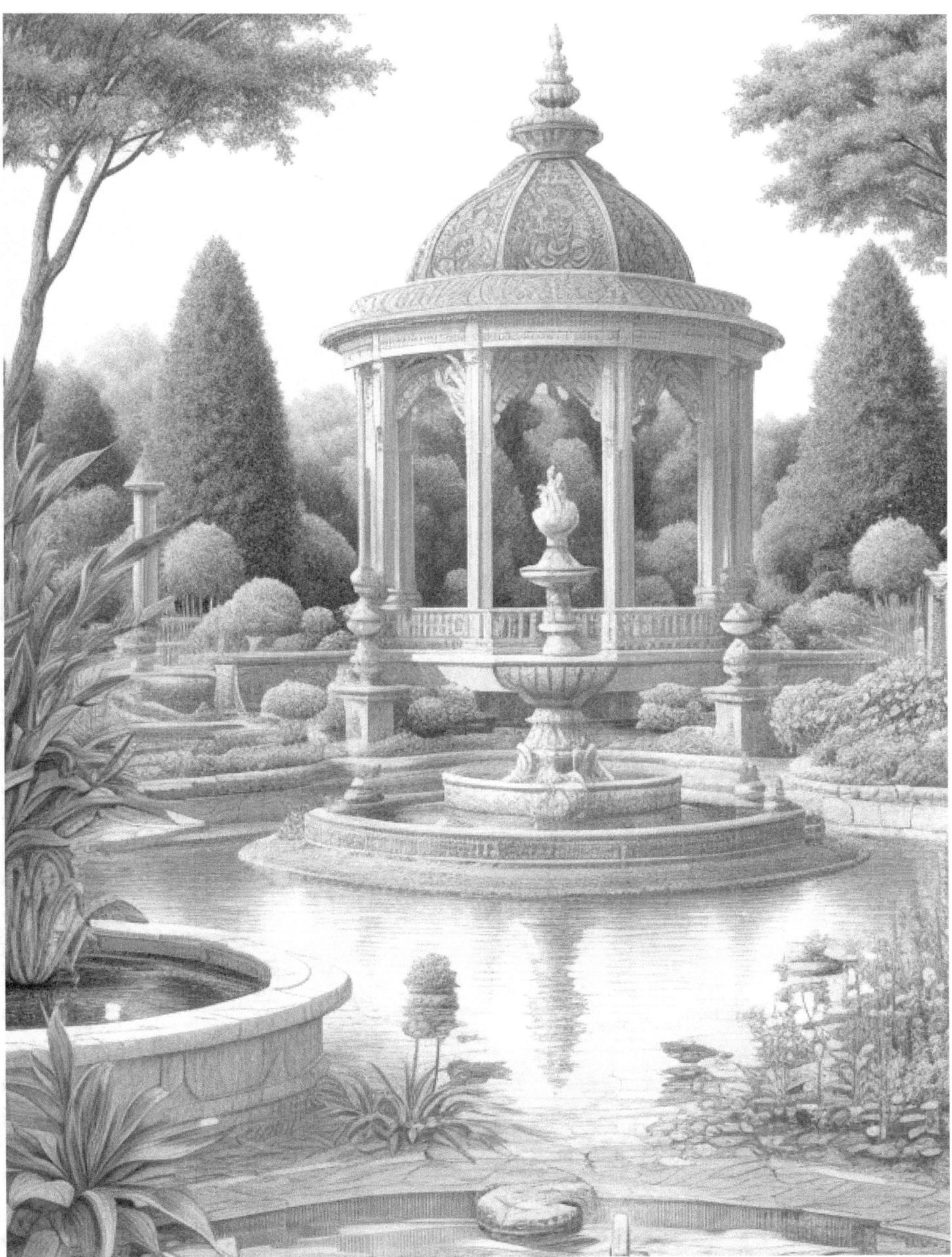

This Page is Intentionally Left Blank to Prevent Bleed Through.

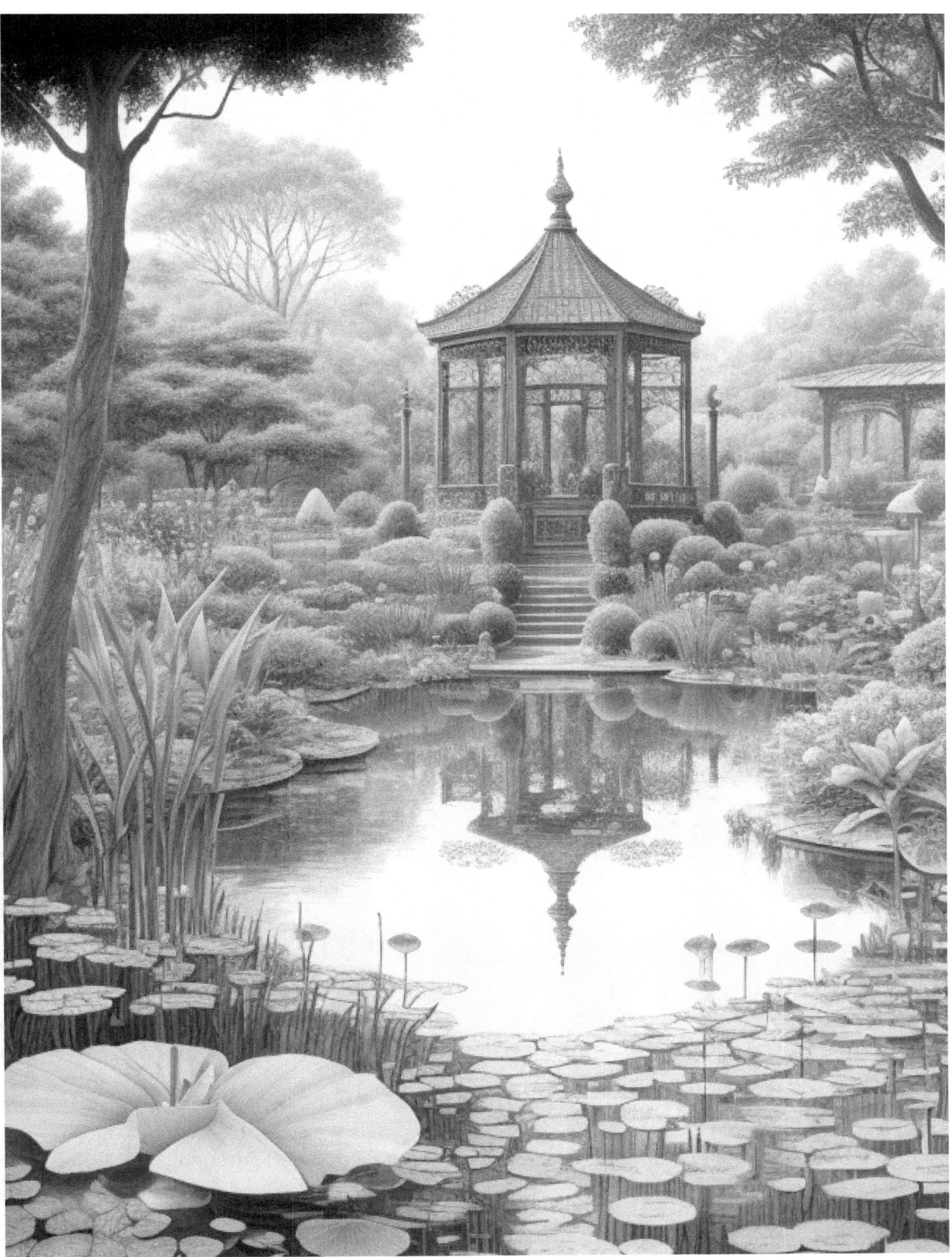

This Page is Intentionally Left Blank to Prevent Bleed Through.

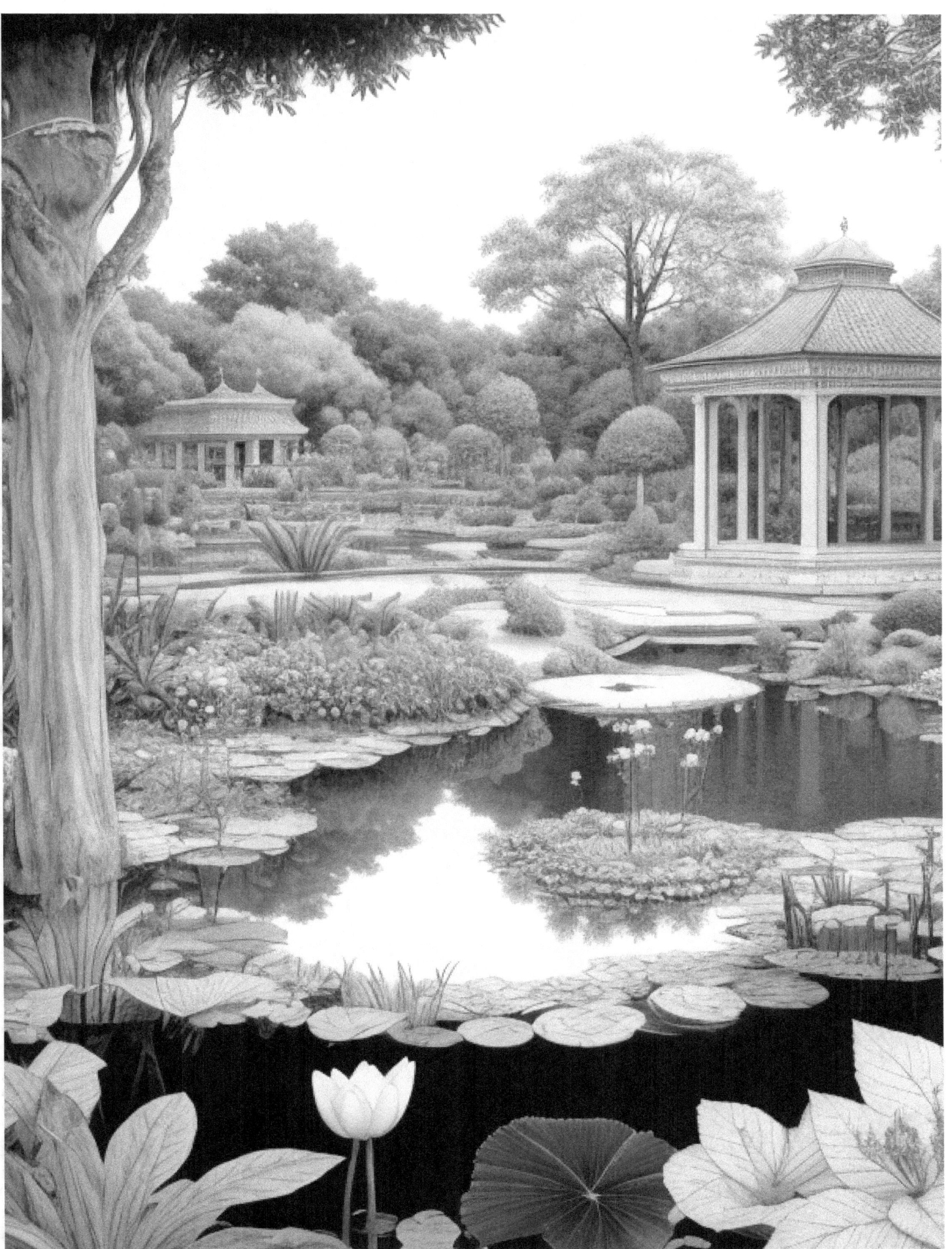

This Page is Intentionally Left Blank to Prevent Bleed Through.

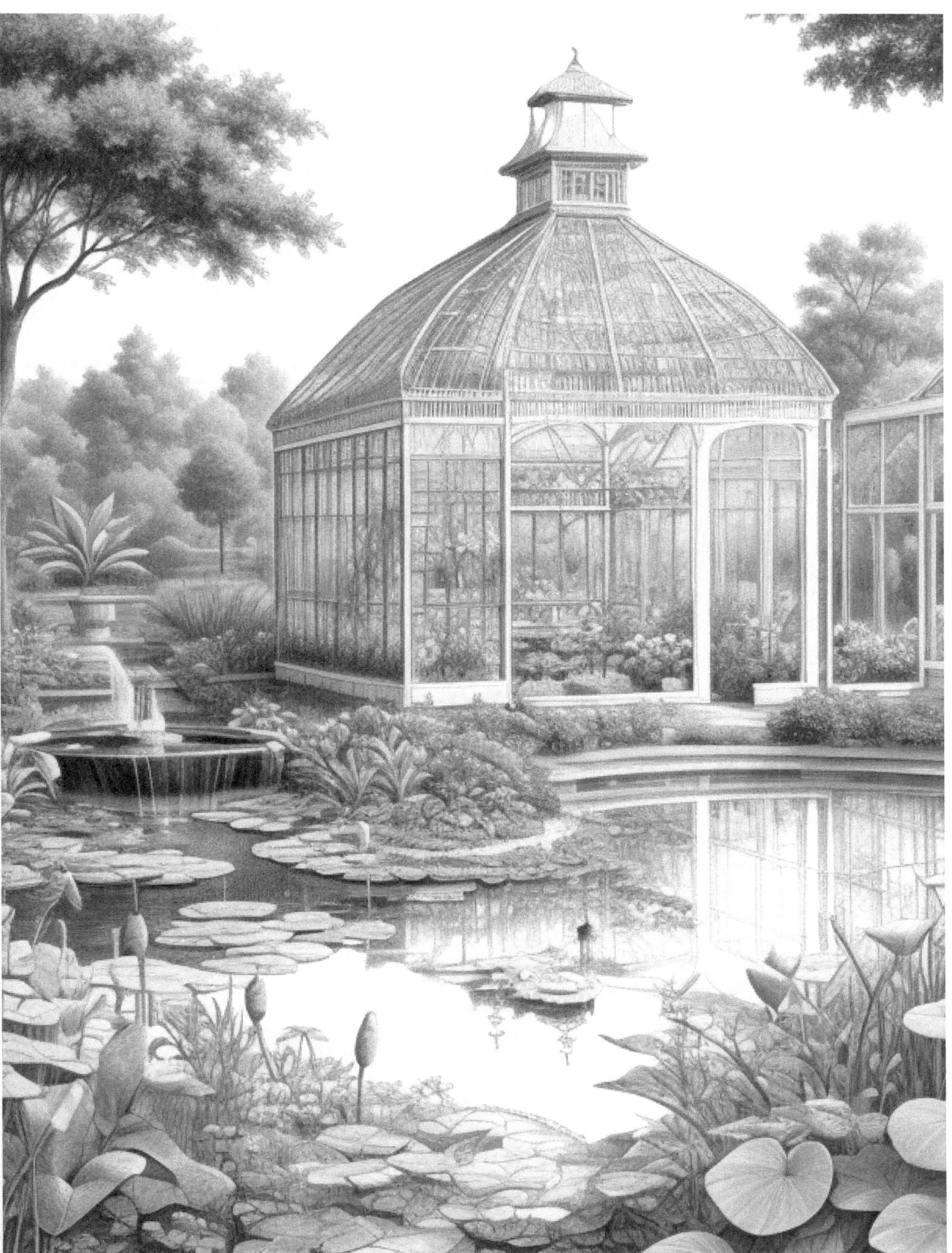

This Page is Intentionally Left Blank to Prevent Bleed Through.

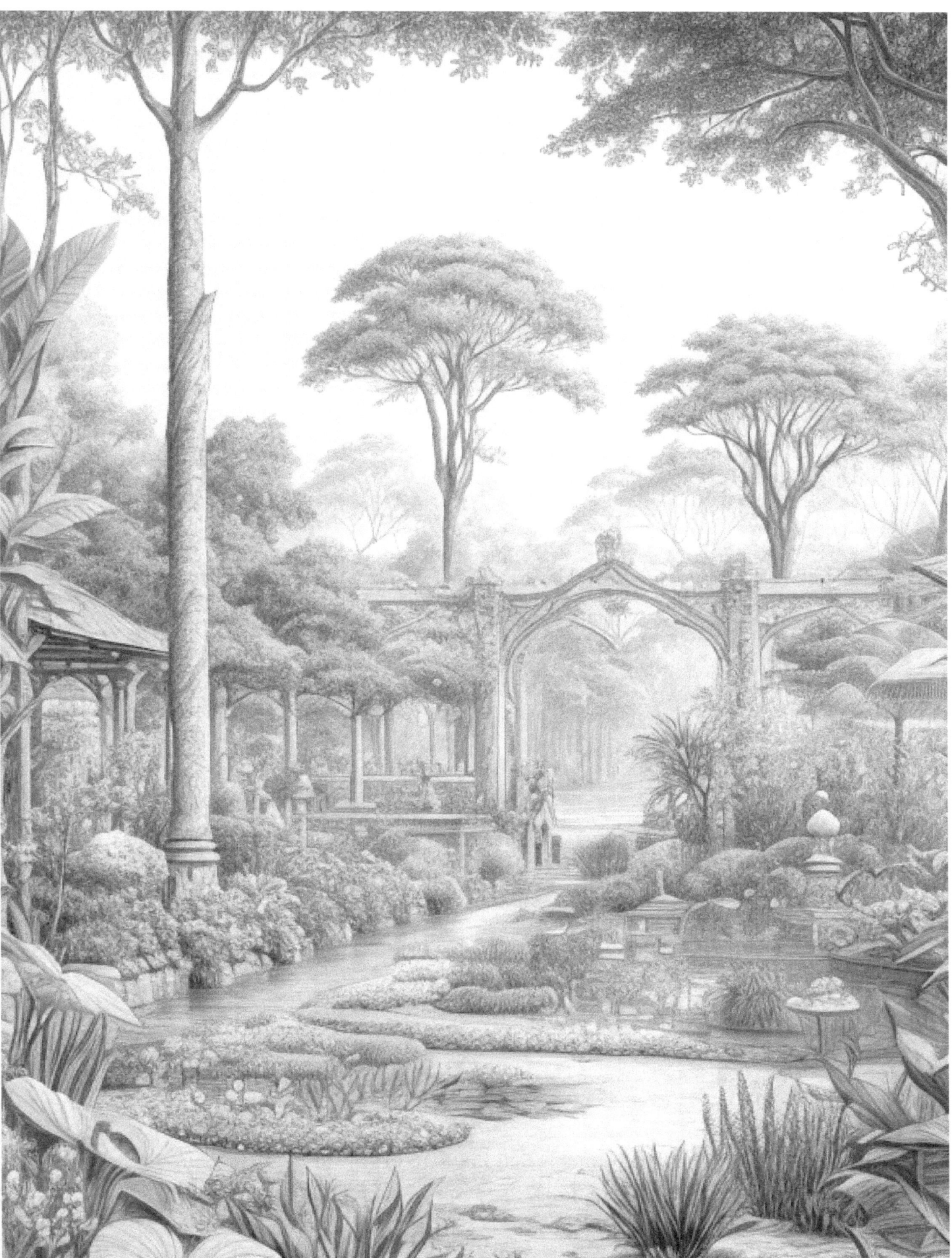

This Page is Intentionally Left Blank to Prevent Bleed Through.

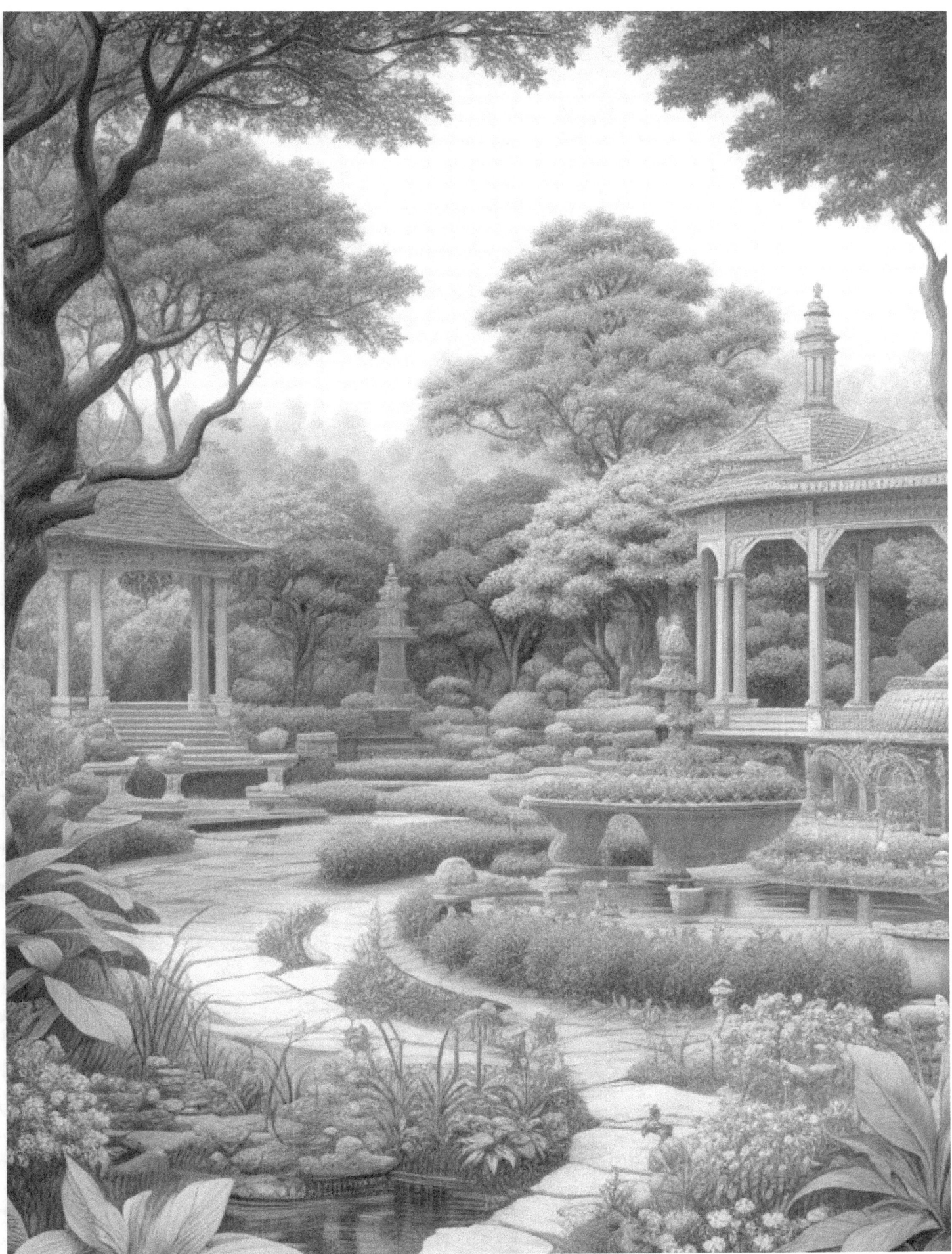

This Page is Intentionally Left Blank to Prevent Bleed Through.

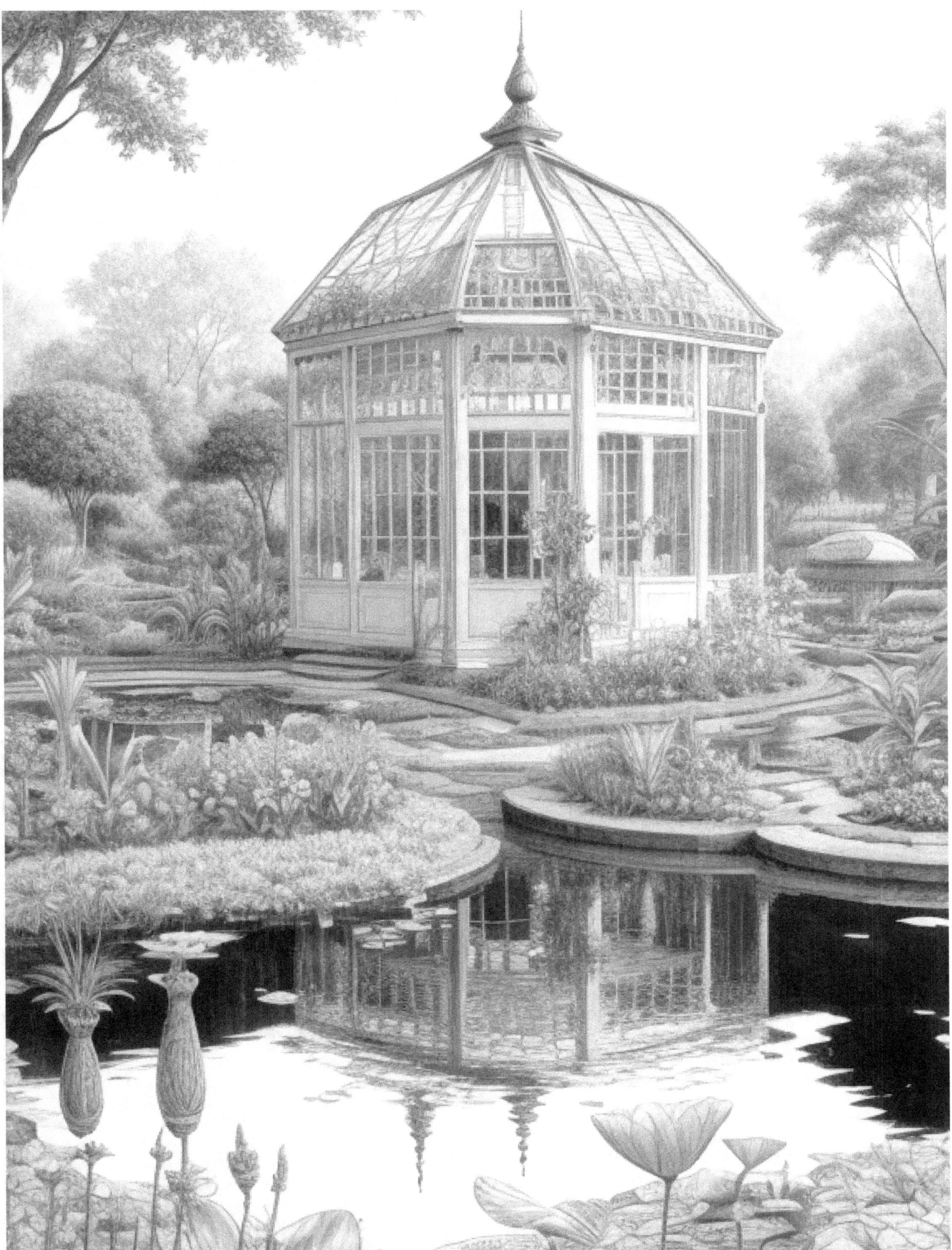

This Page is Intentionally Left Blank to Prevent Bleed Through.

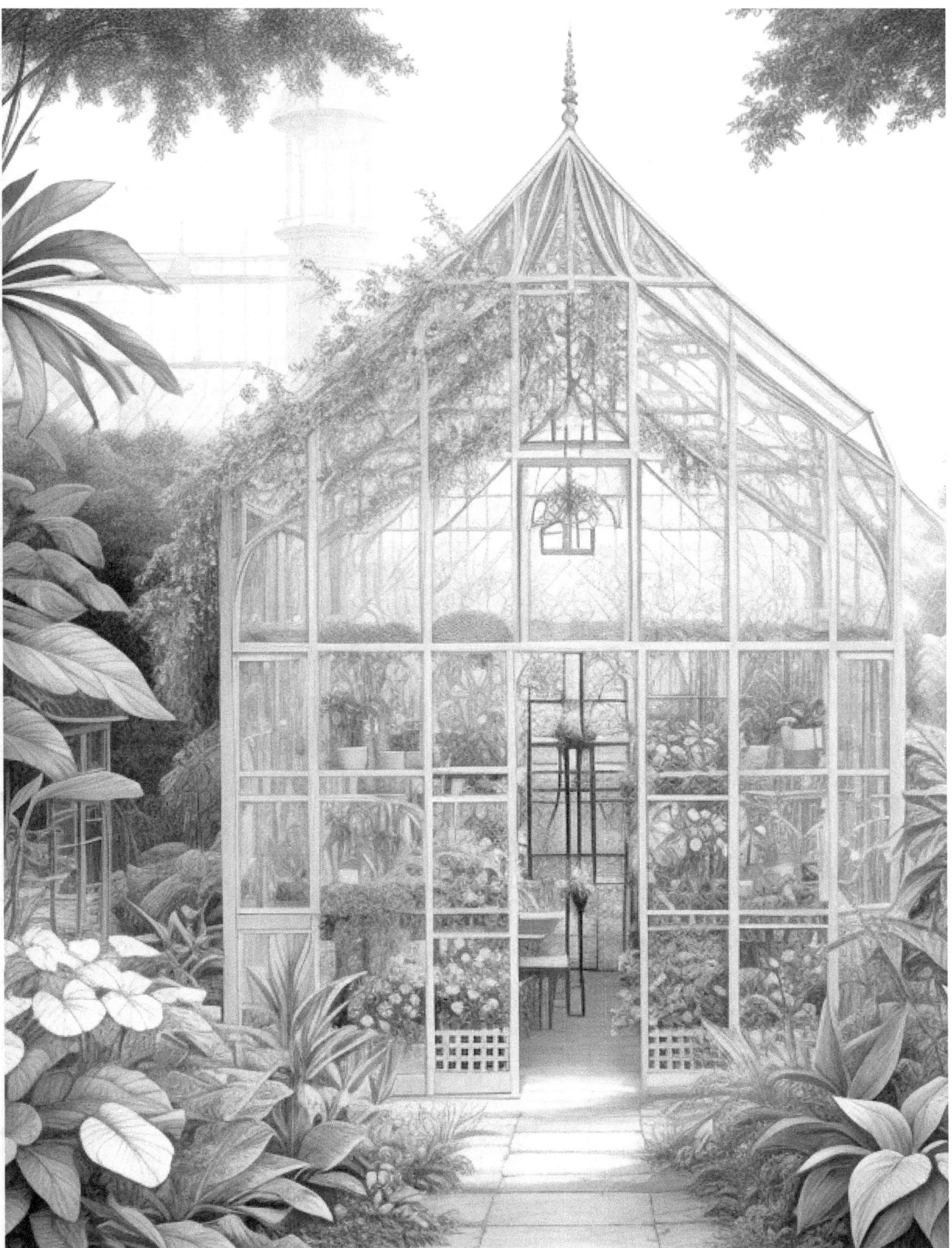

This Page is Intentionally Left Blank to Prevent Bleed Through.

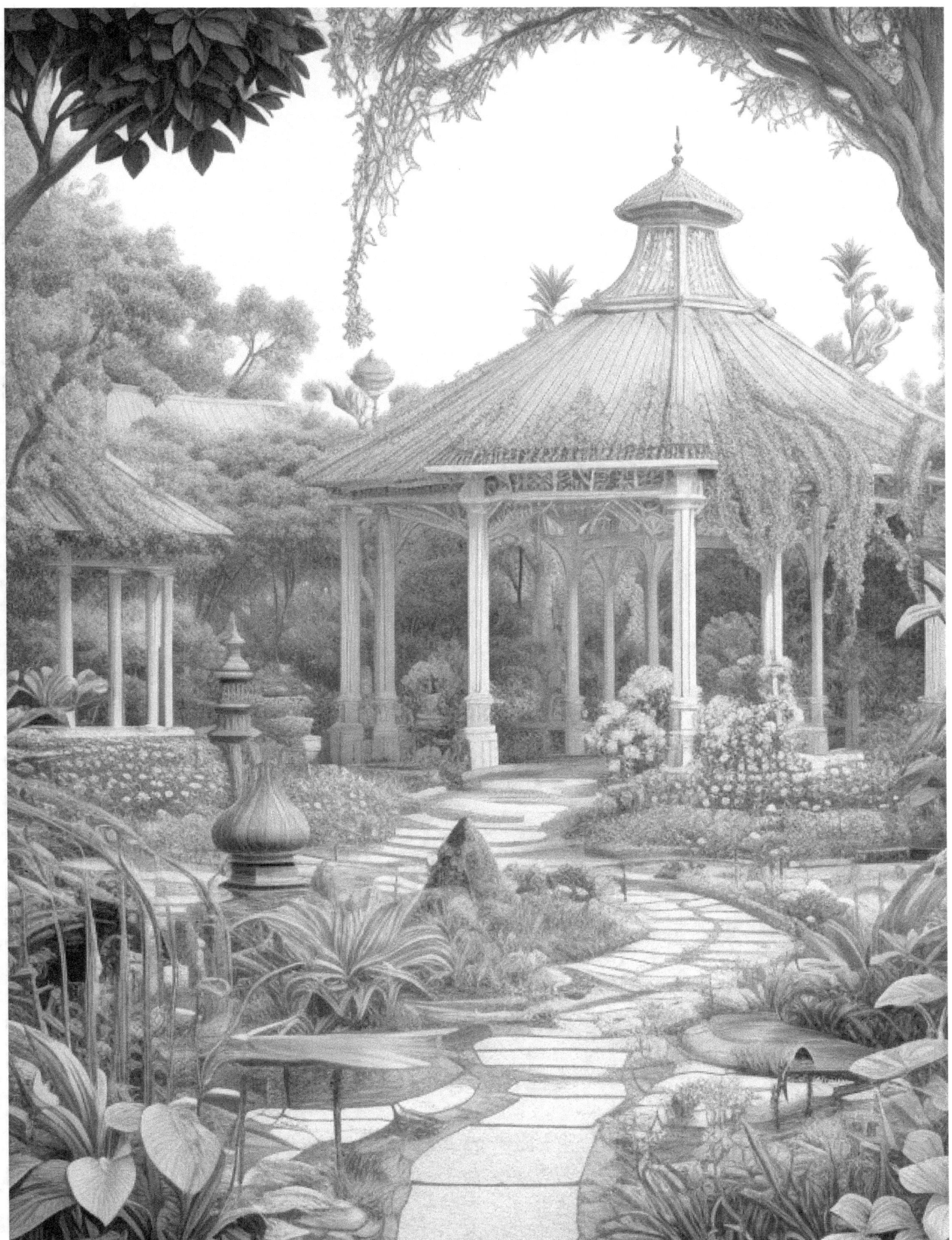

This Page is Intentionally Left Blank to Prevent Bleed Through.

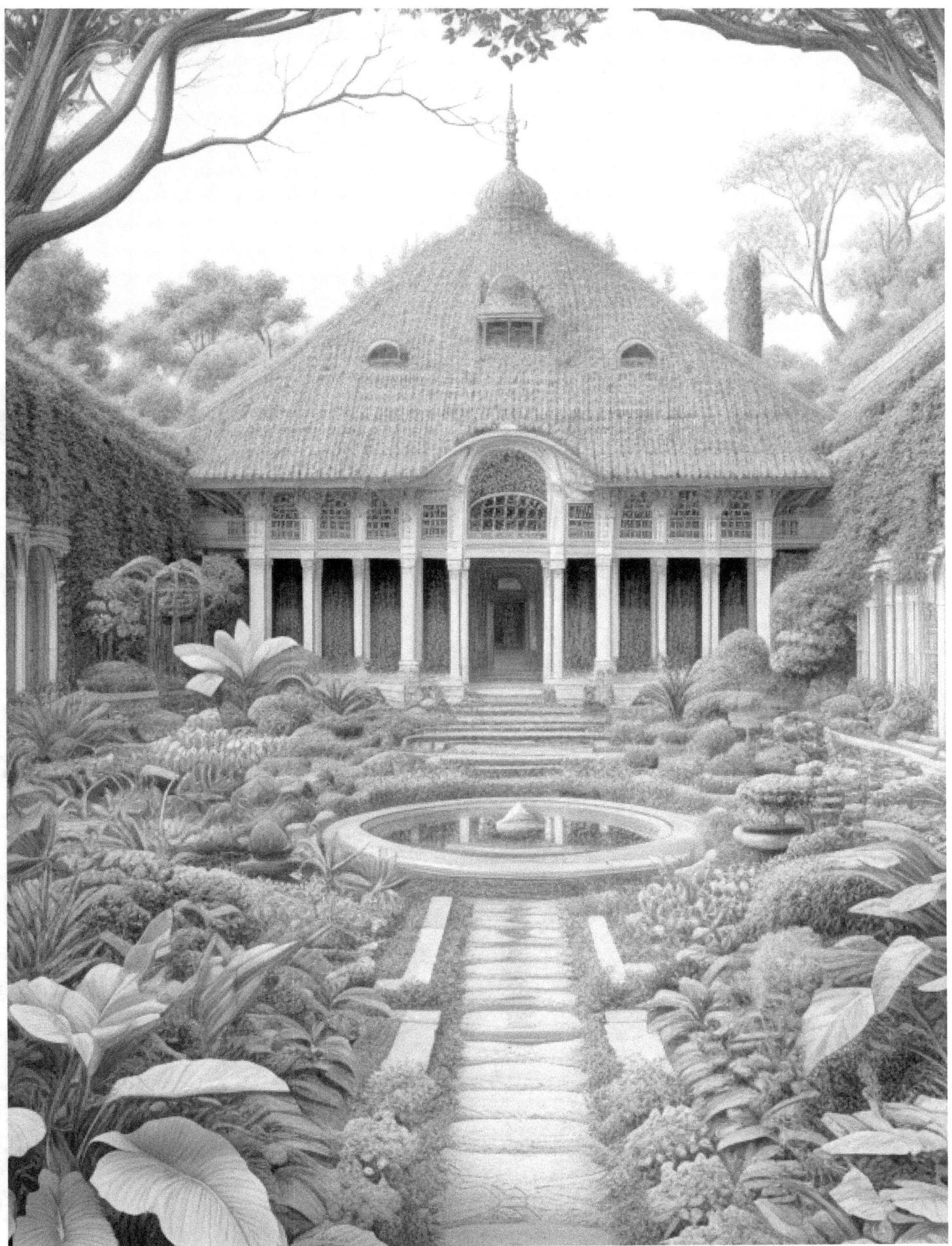

This Page is Intentionally Left Blank to Prevent Bleed Through.

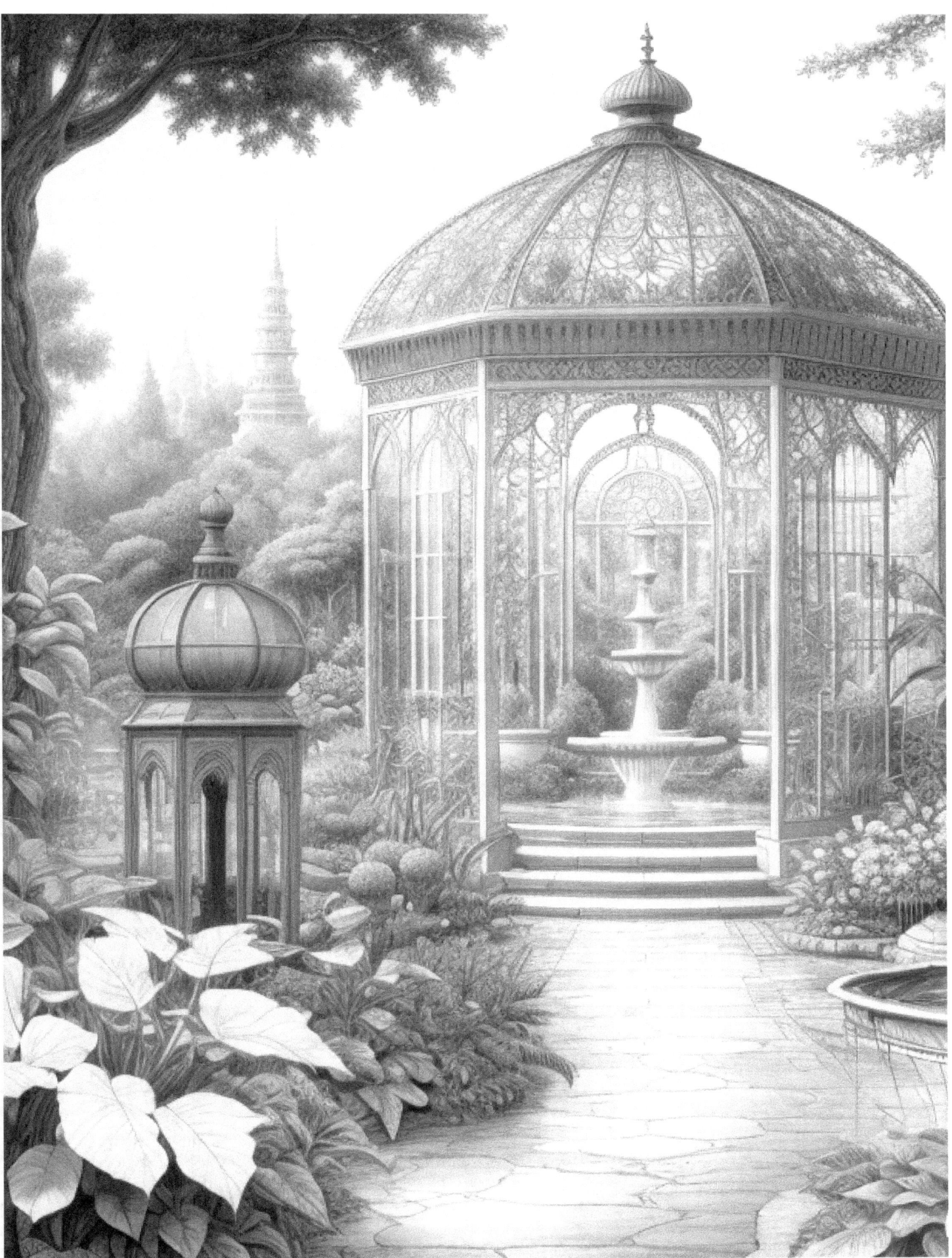

This Page is Intentionally Left Blank to Prevent Bleed Through.

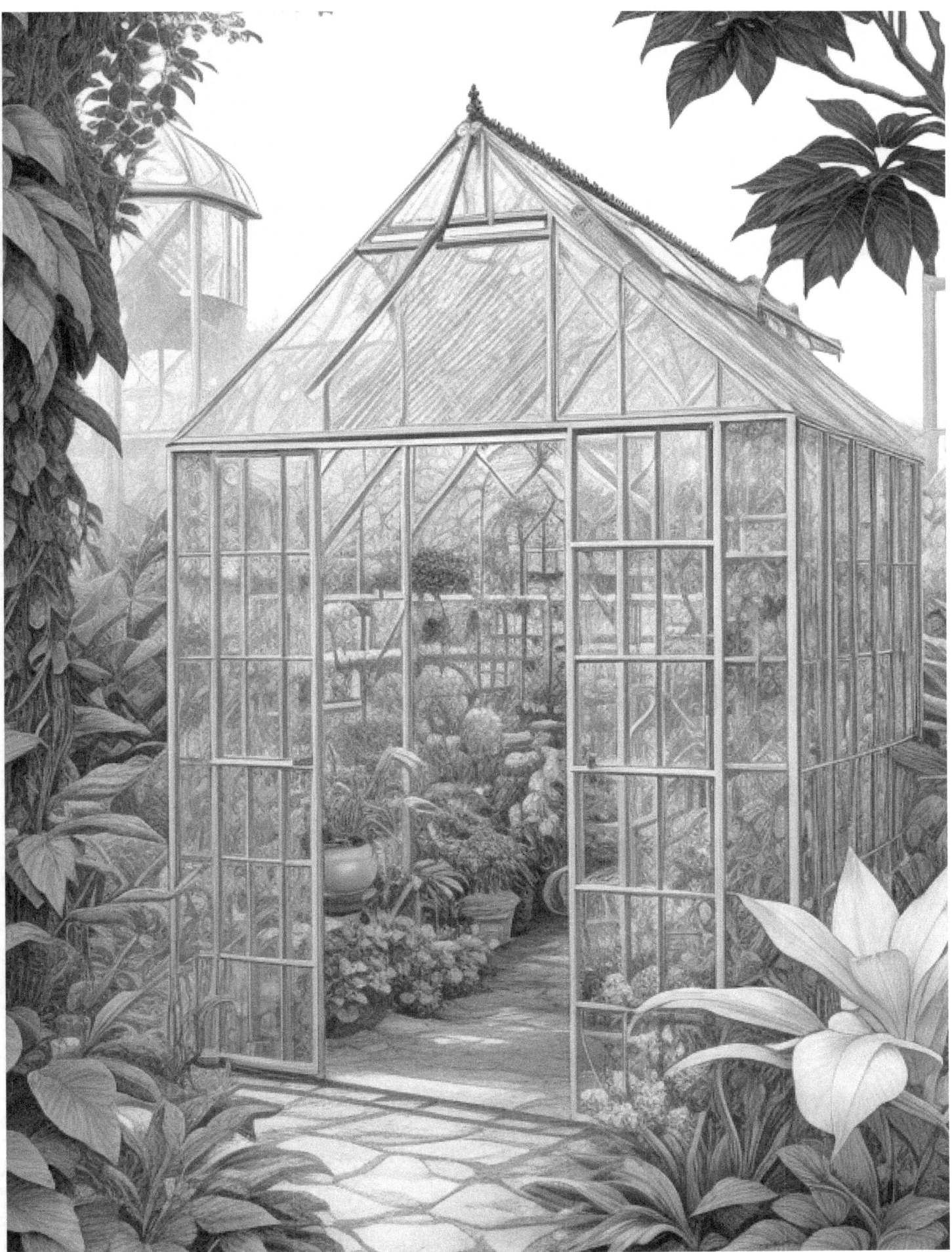

This Page is Intentionally Left Blank to Prevent Bleed Through.

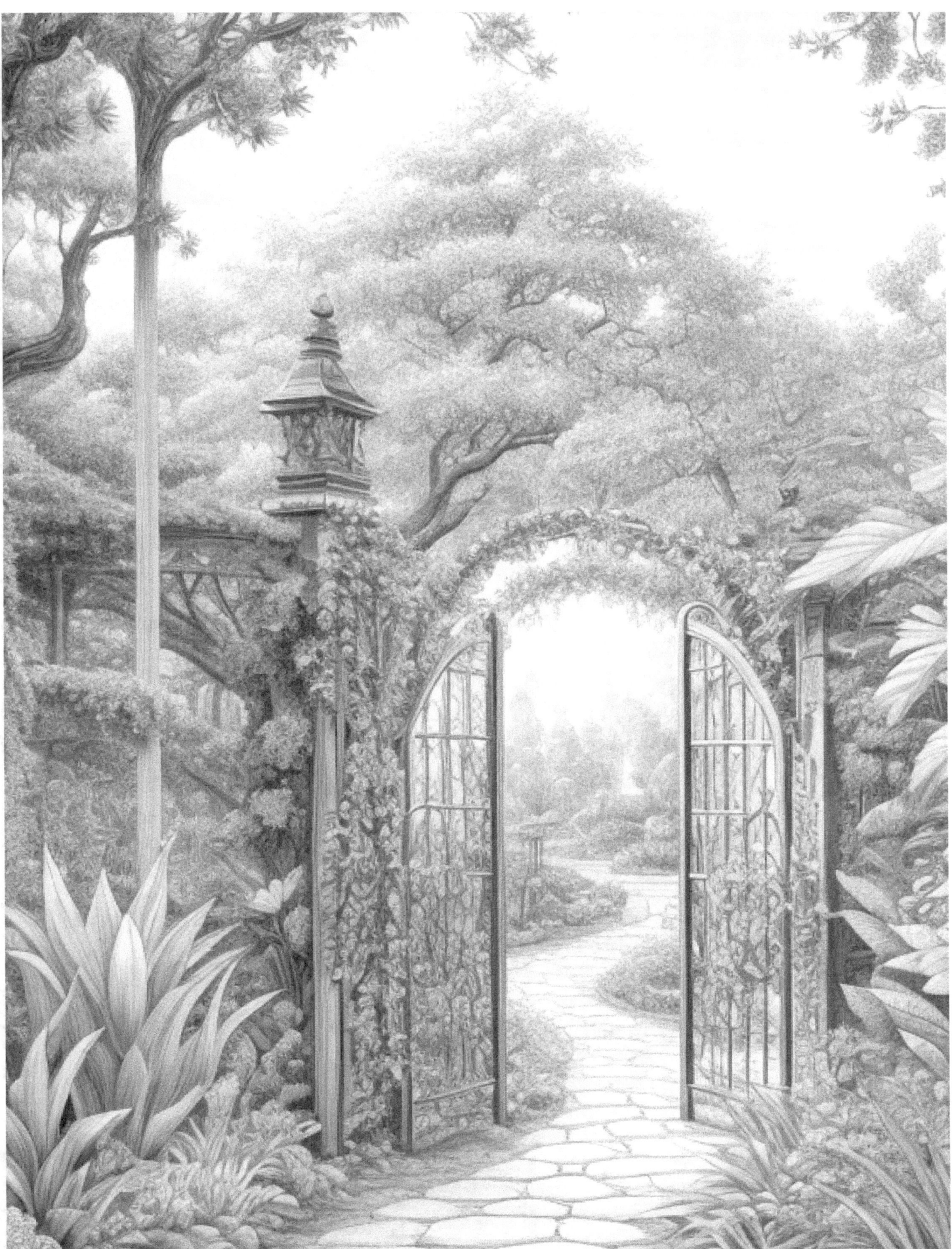

This Page is Intentionally Left Blank to Prevent Bleed Through.

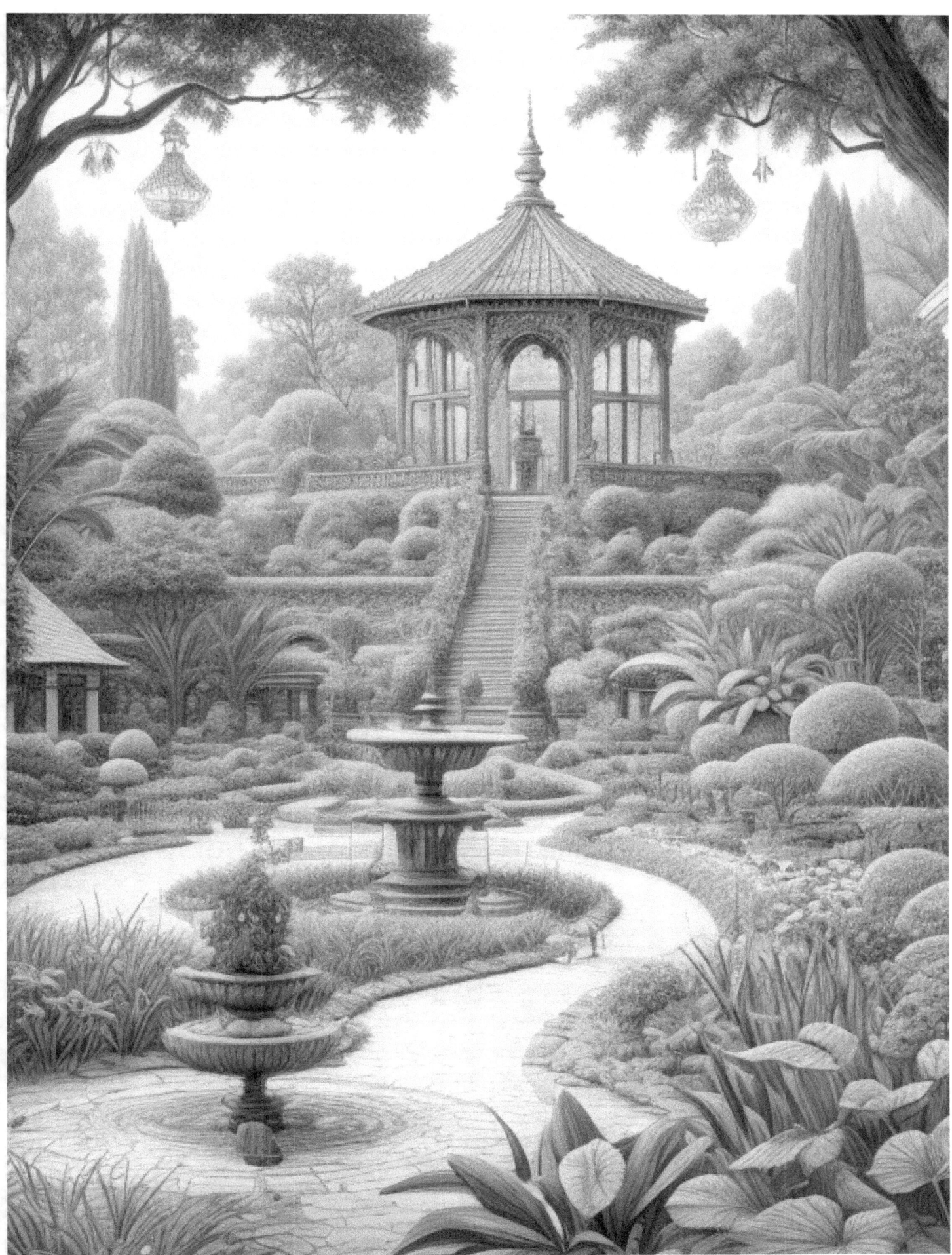

This Page is Intentionally Left Blank to Prevent Bleed Through.

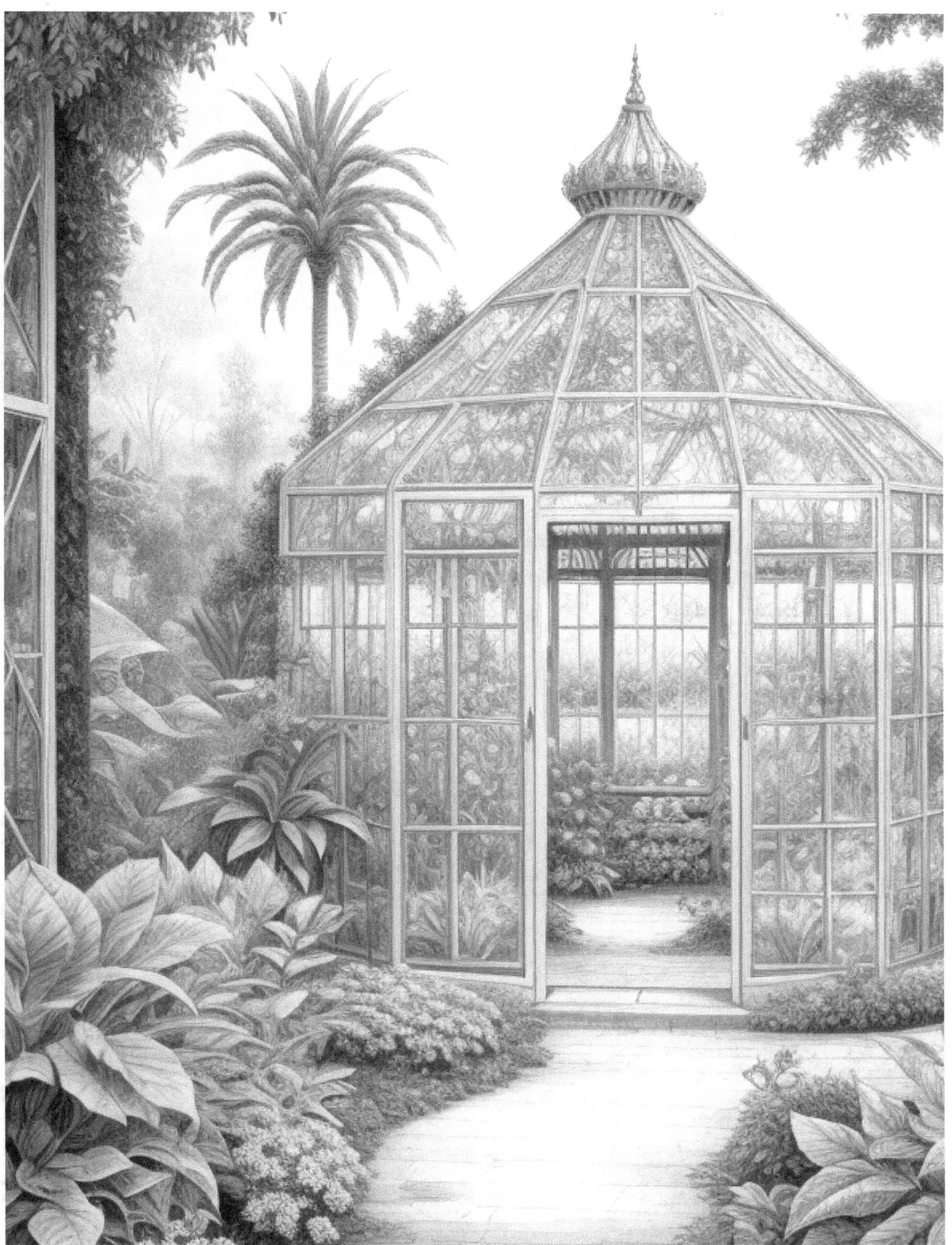

This Page is Intentionally Left Blank to Prevent Bleed Through.

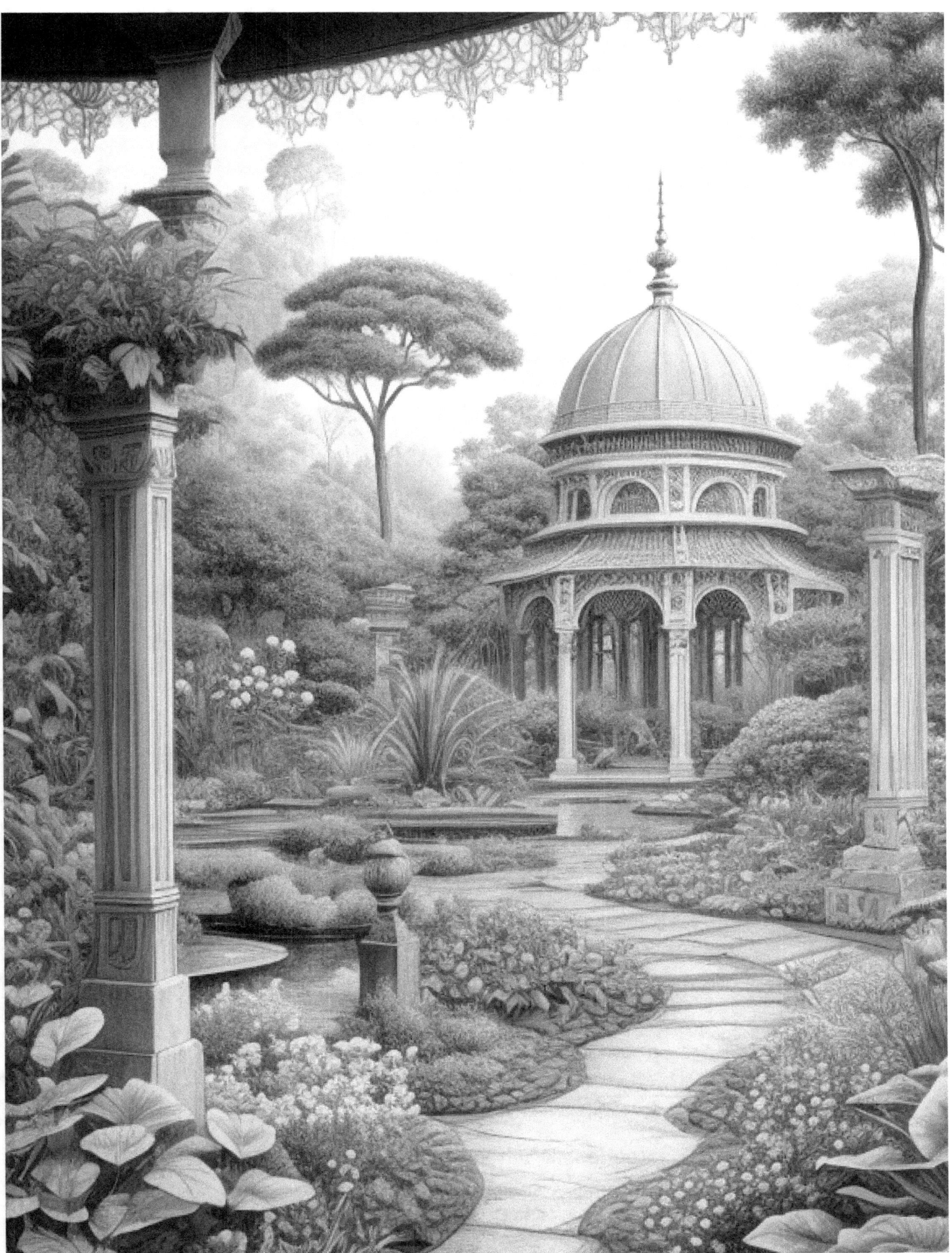

This Page is Intentionally Left Blank to Prevent Bleed Through.

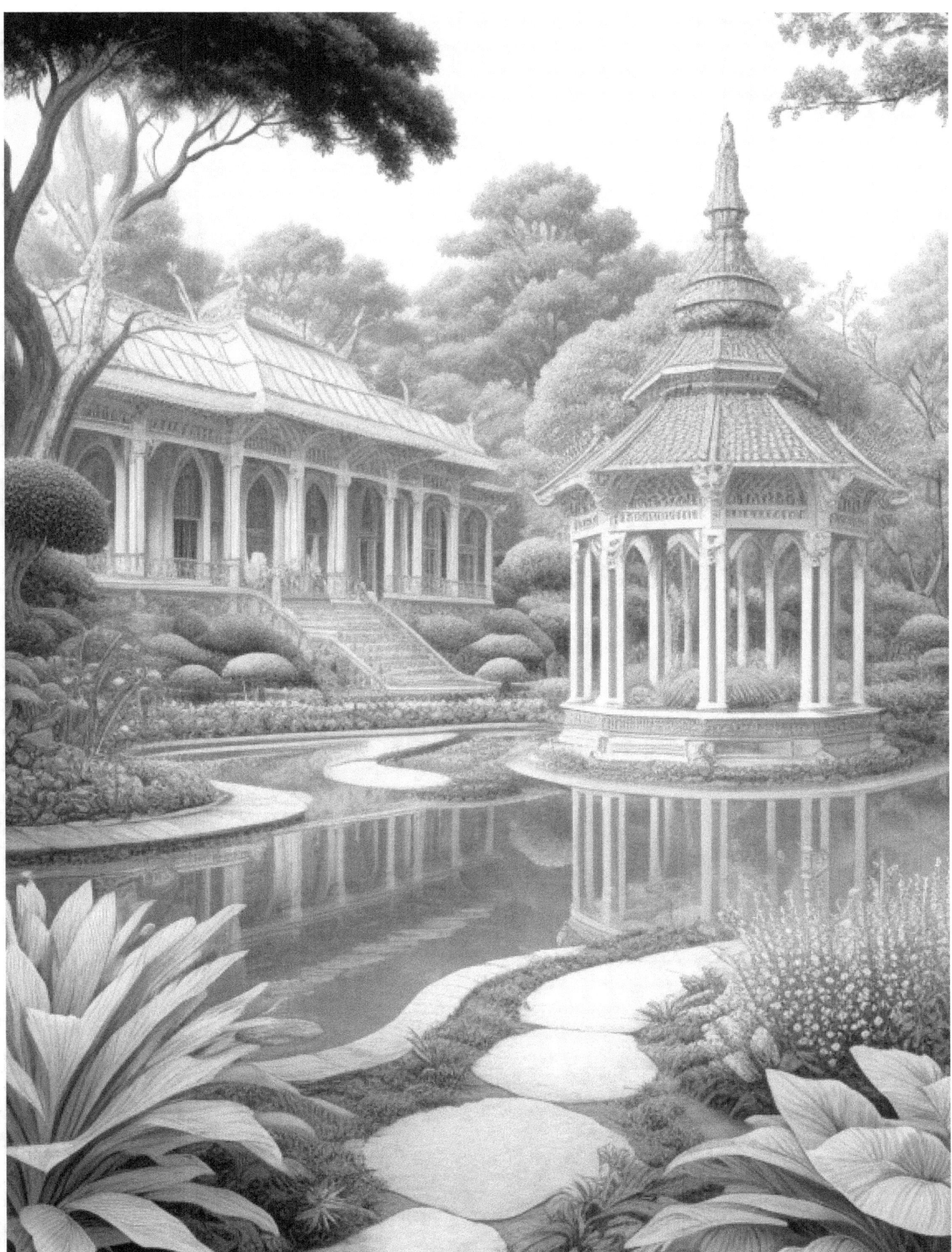

This Page is Intentionally Left Blank to Prevent Bleed Through.

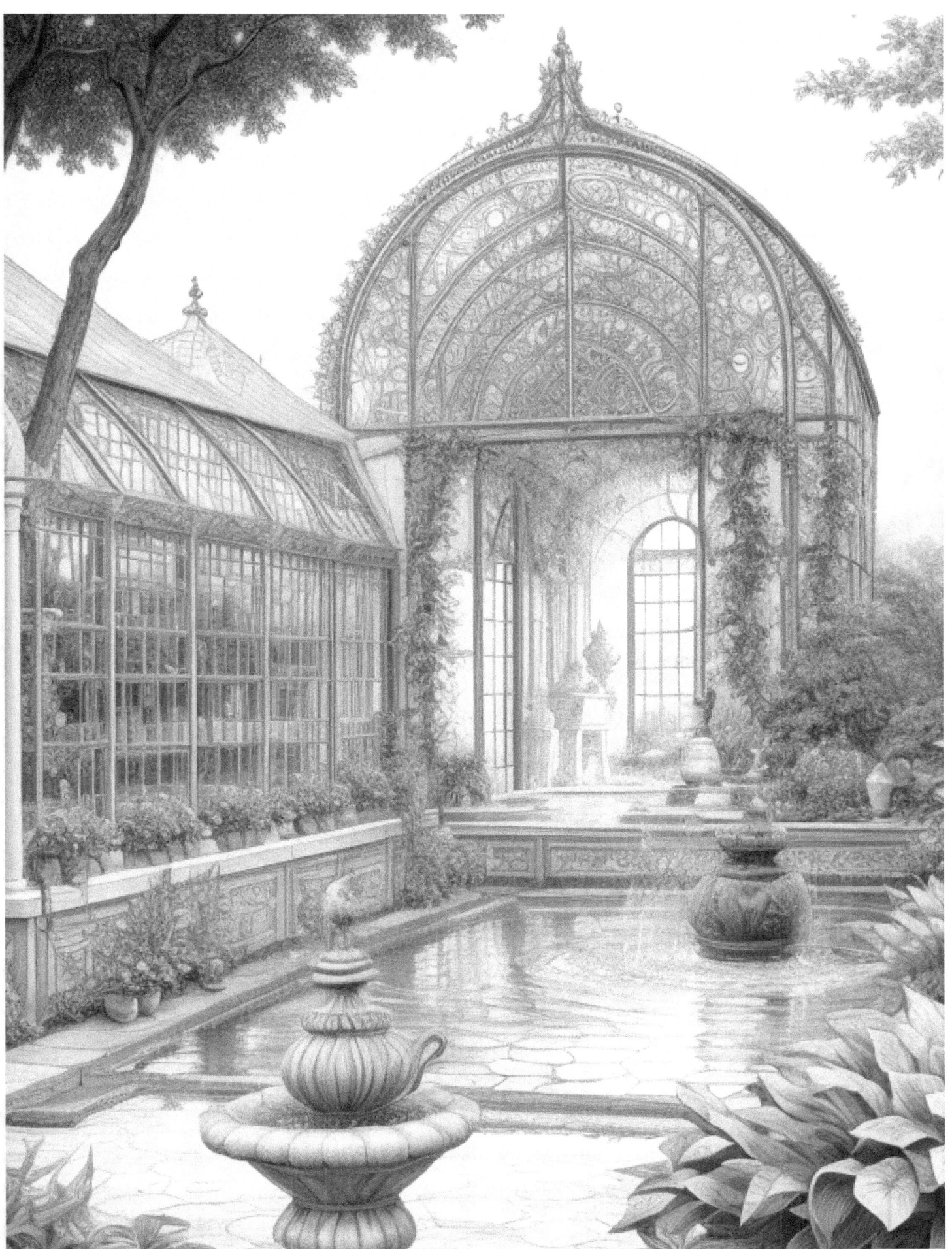

This Page is Intentionally Left Blank to Prevent Bleed Through.

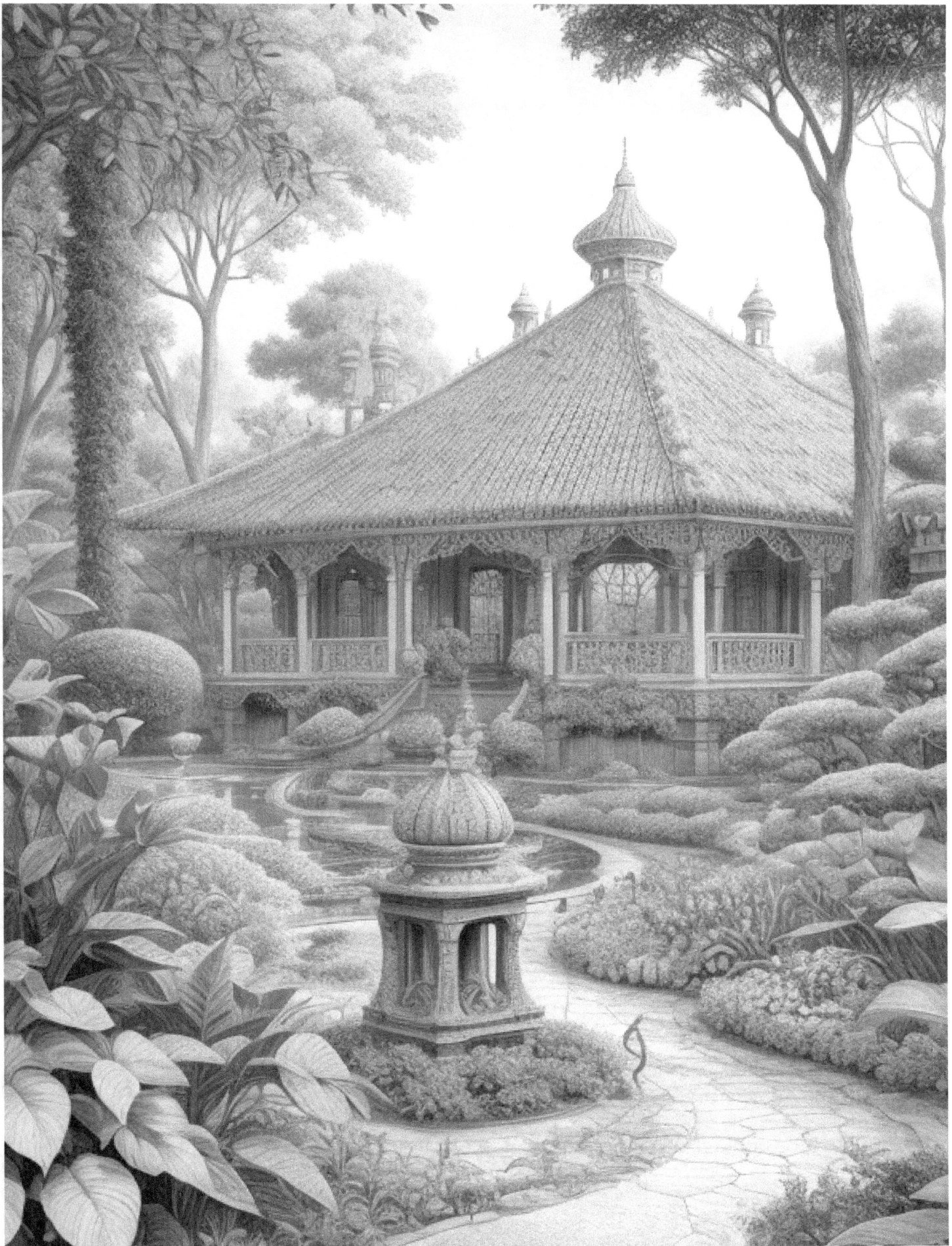

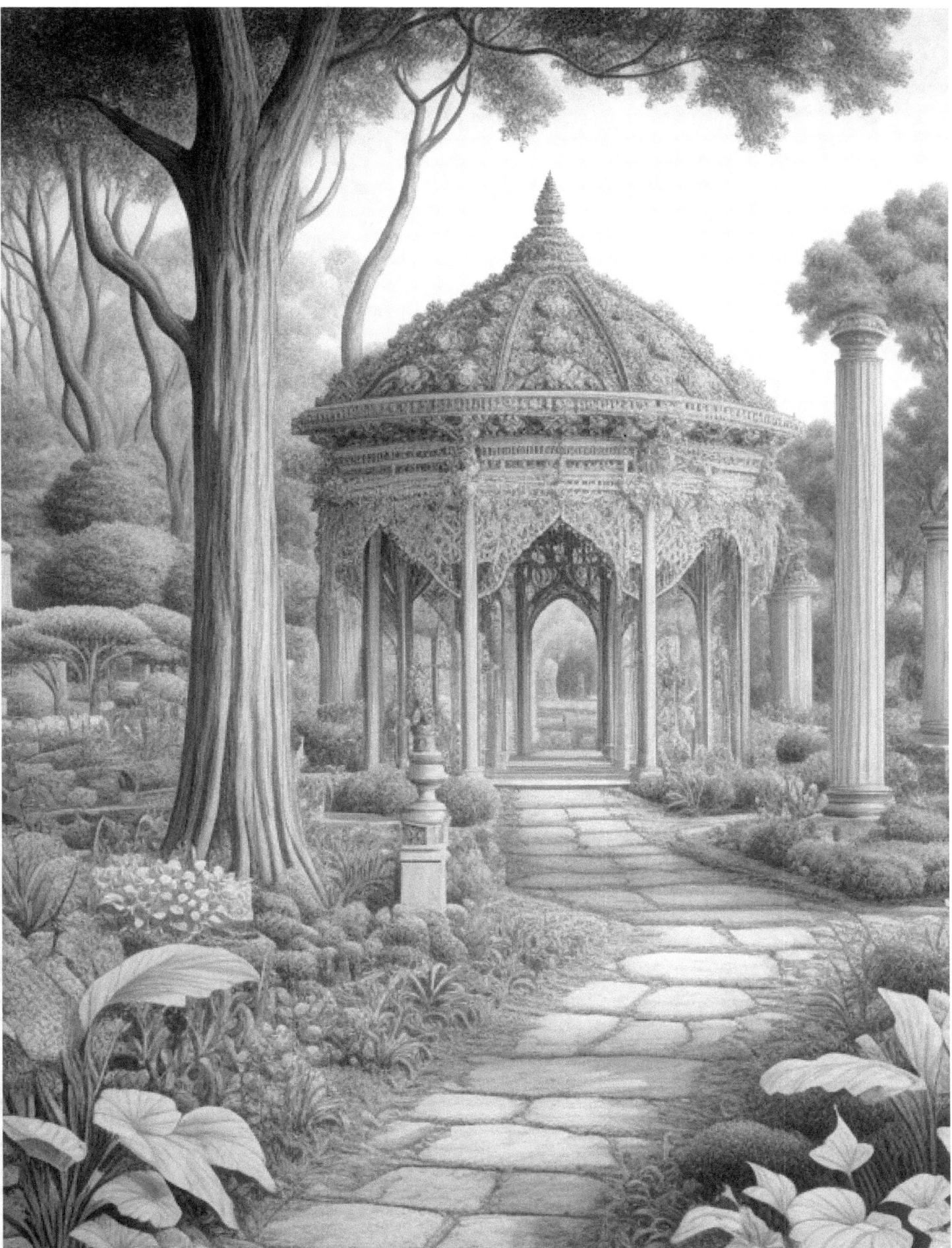

This Page is Intentionally Left Blank to Prevent Bleed Through.

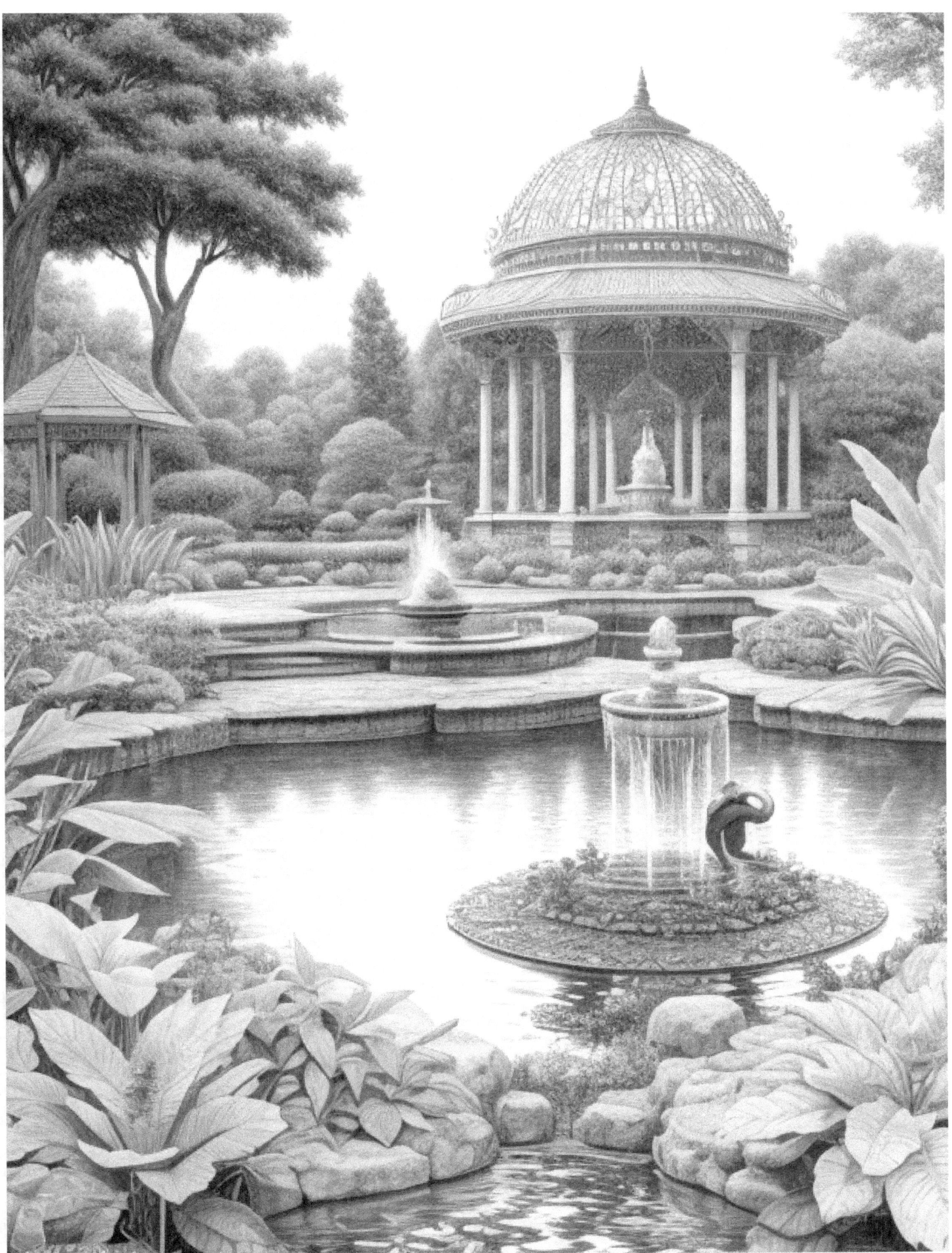

This Page is Intentionally Left Blank to Prevent Bleed Through.

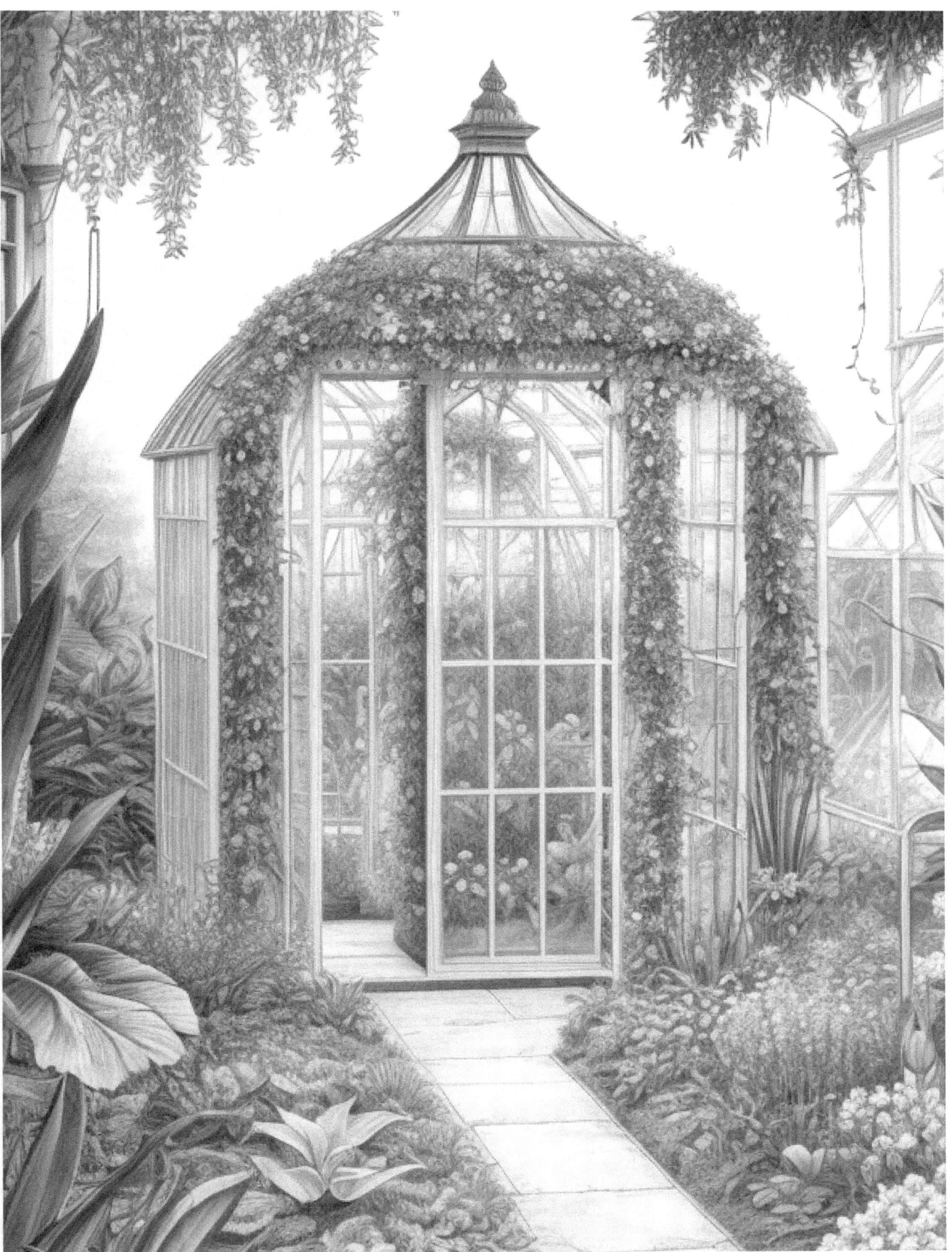

This Page is Intentionally Left Blank to Prevent Bleed Through.

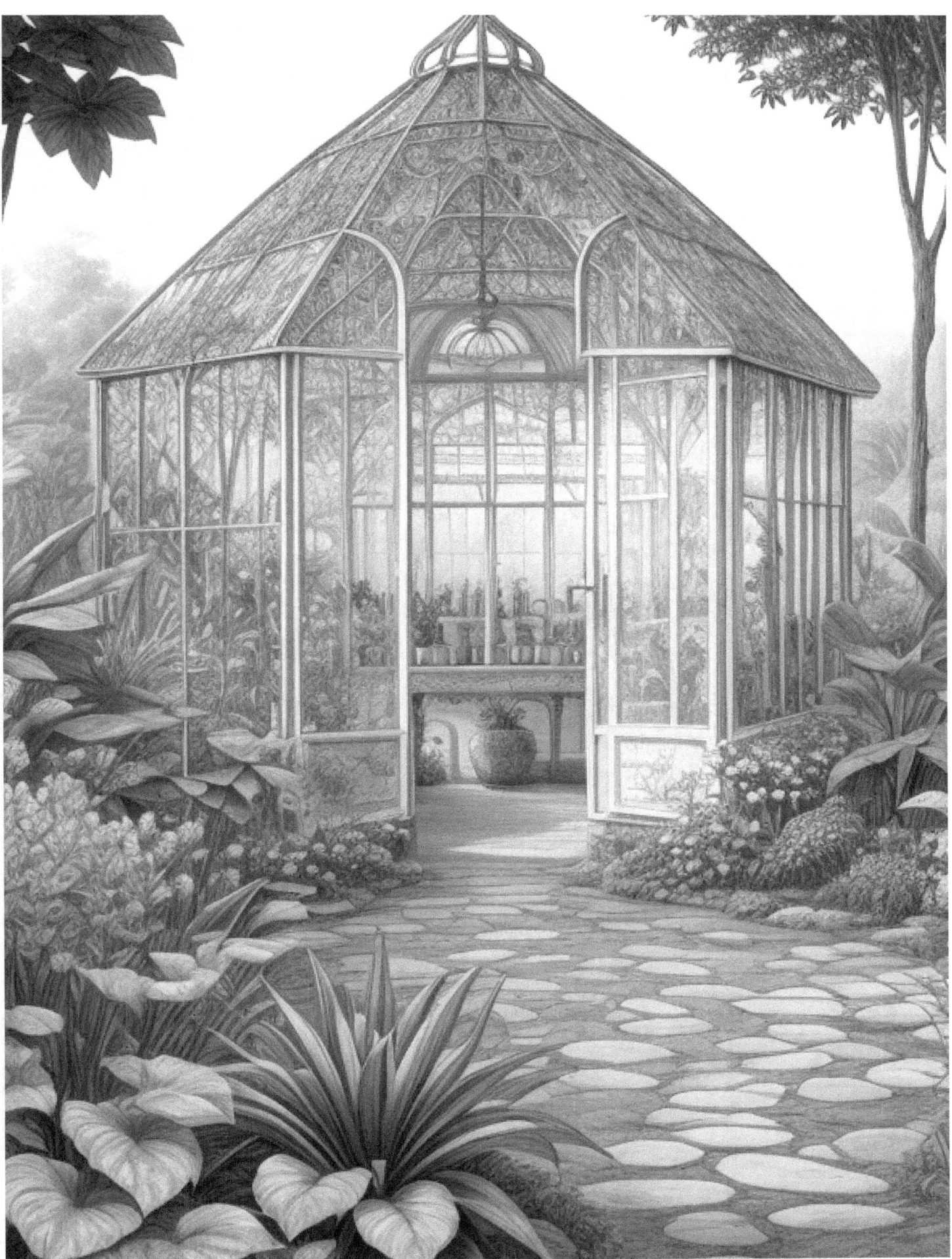

This Page is Intentionally Left Blank to Prevent Bleed Through.

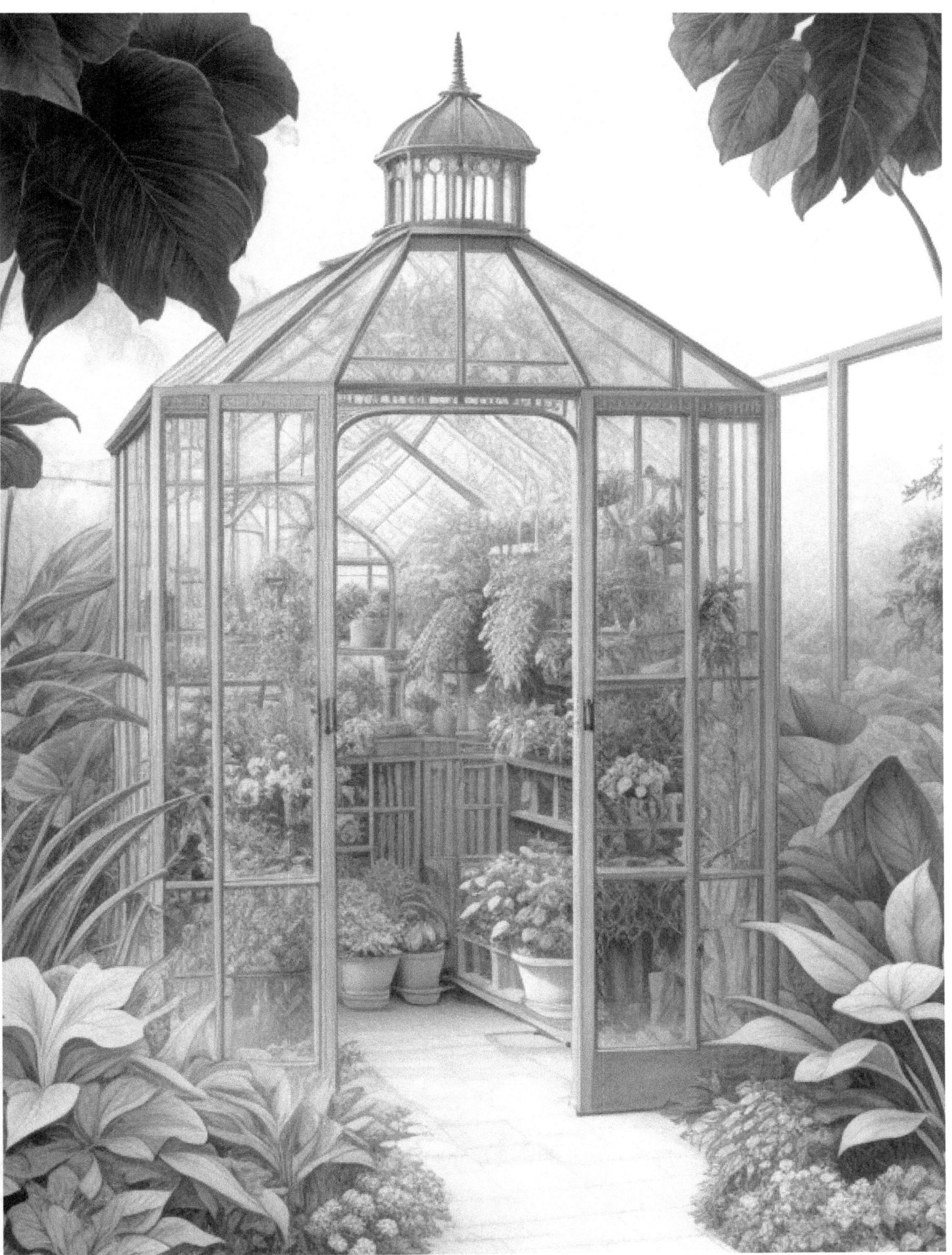

This Page is Intentionally Left Blank to Prevent Bleed Through.

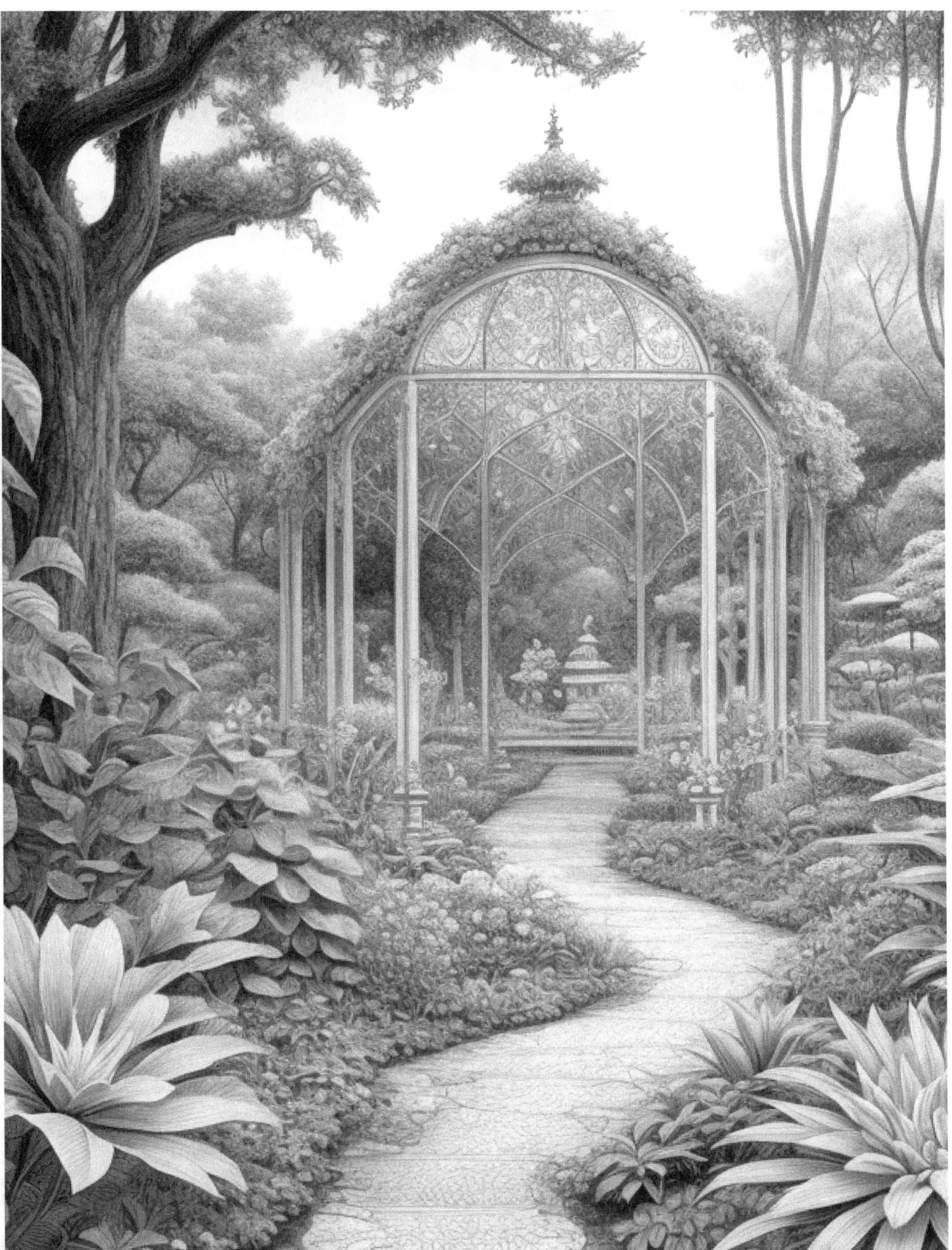

This Page is Intentionally Left Blank to Prevent Bleed Through.

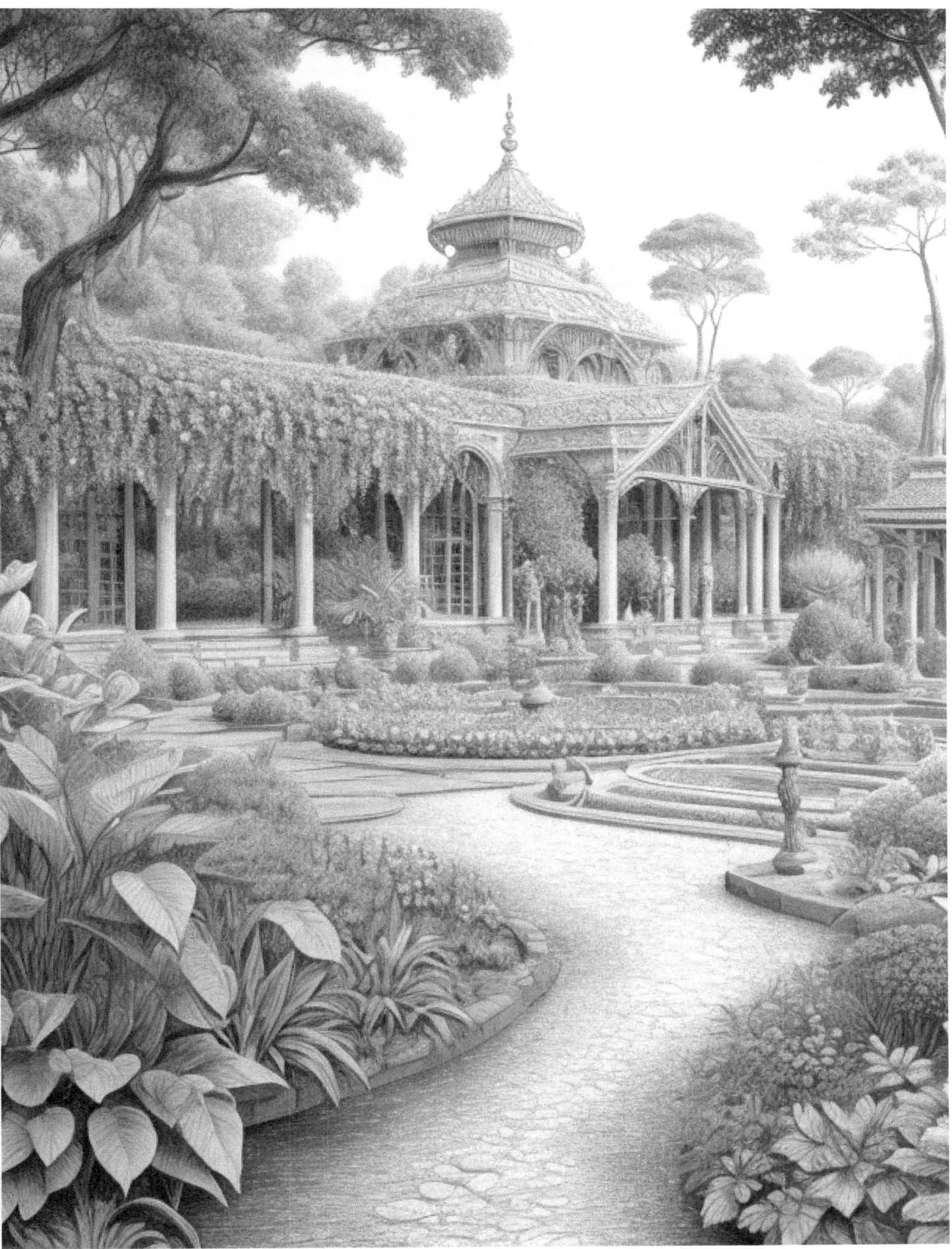

This Page is Intentionally Left Blank to Prevent Bleed Through.

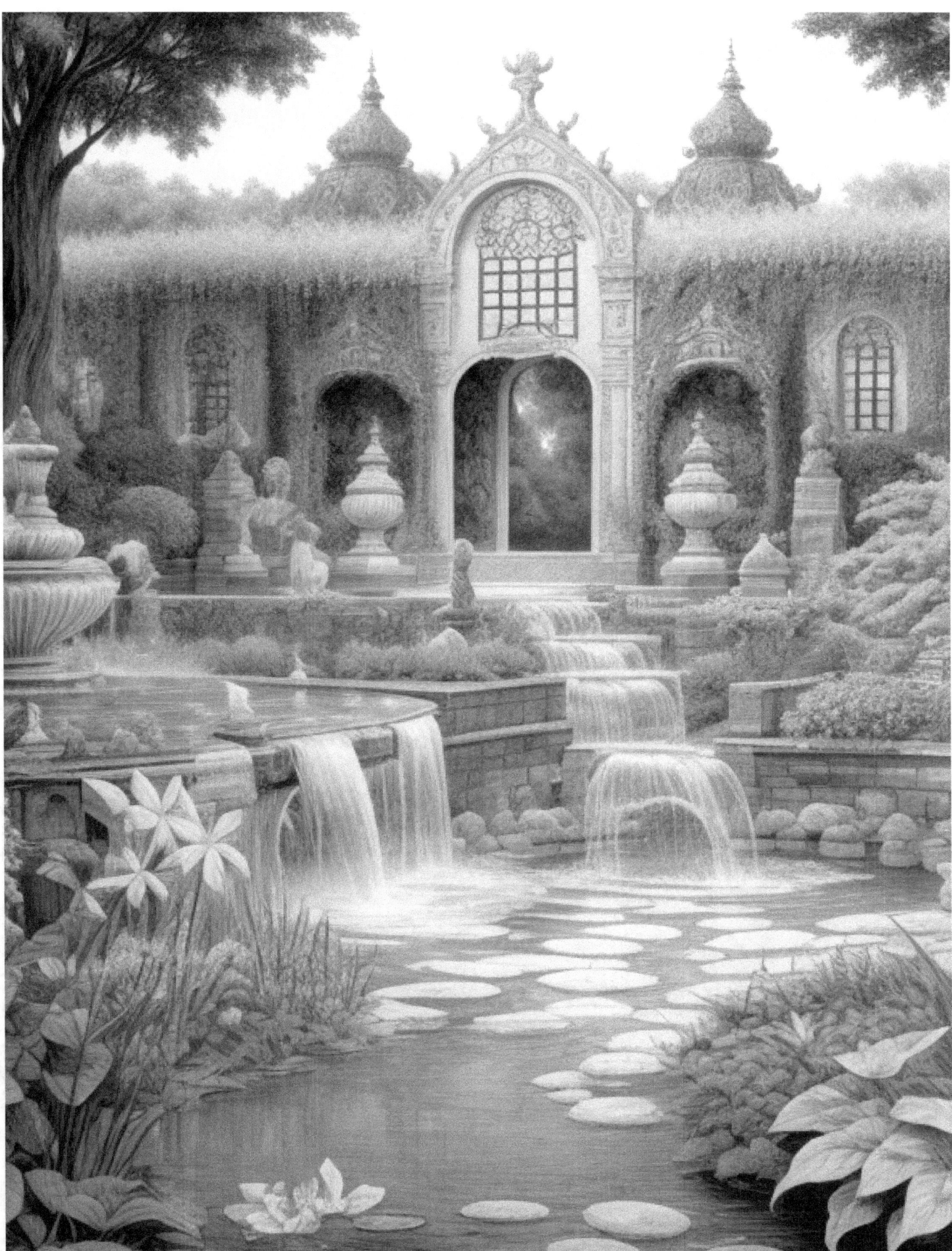

This Page is Intentionally Left Blank to Prevent Bleed Through.

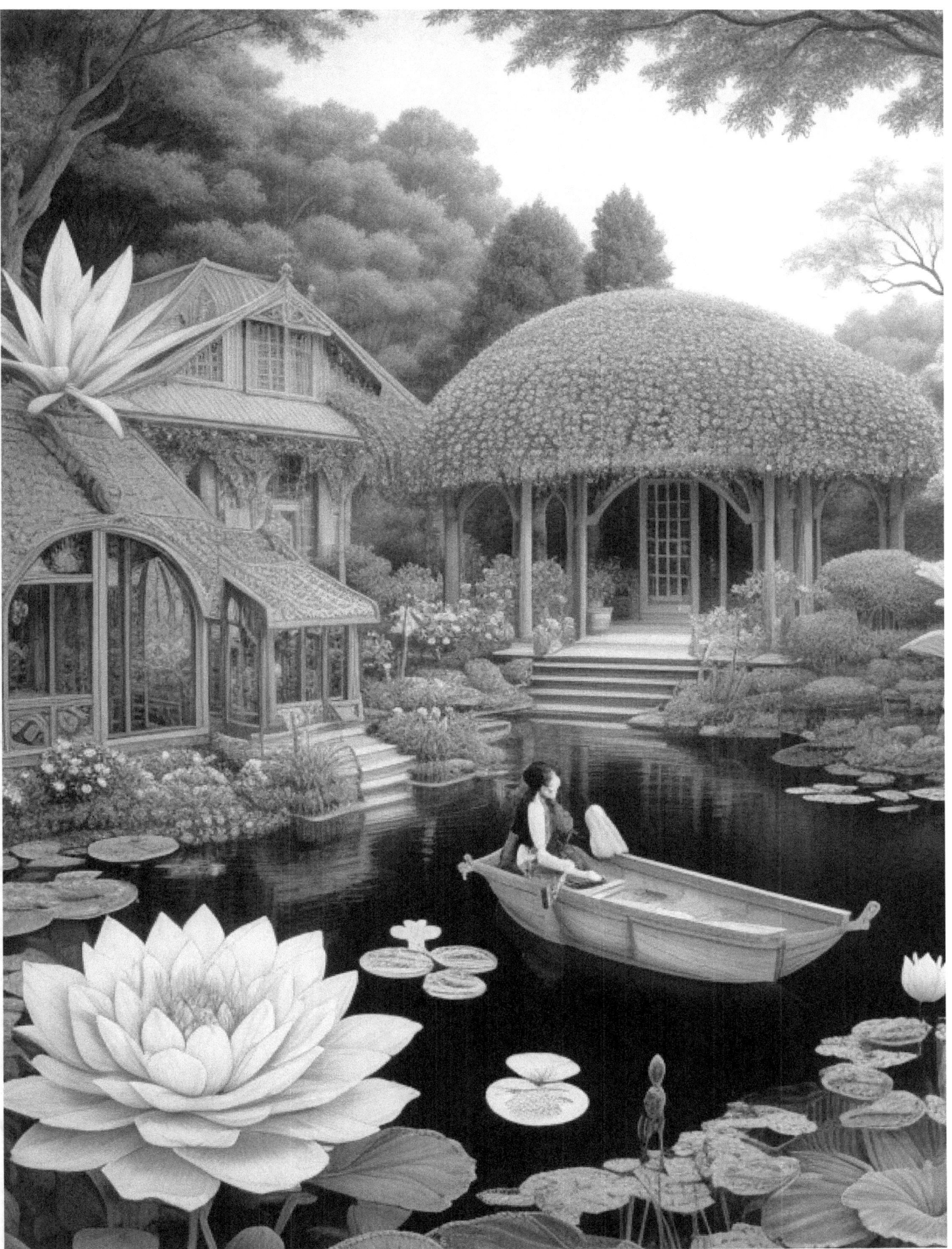

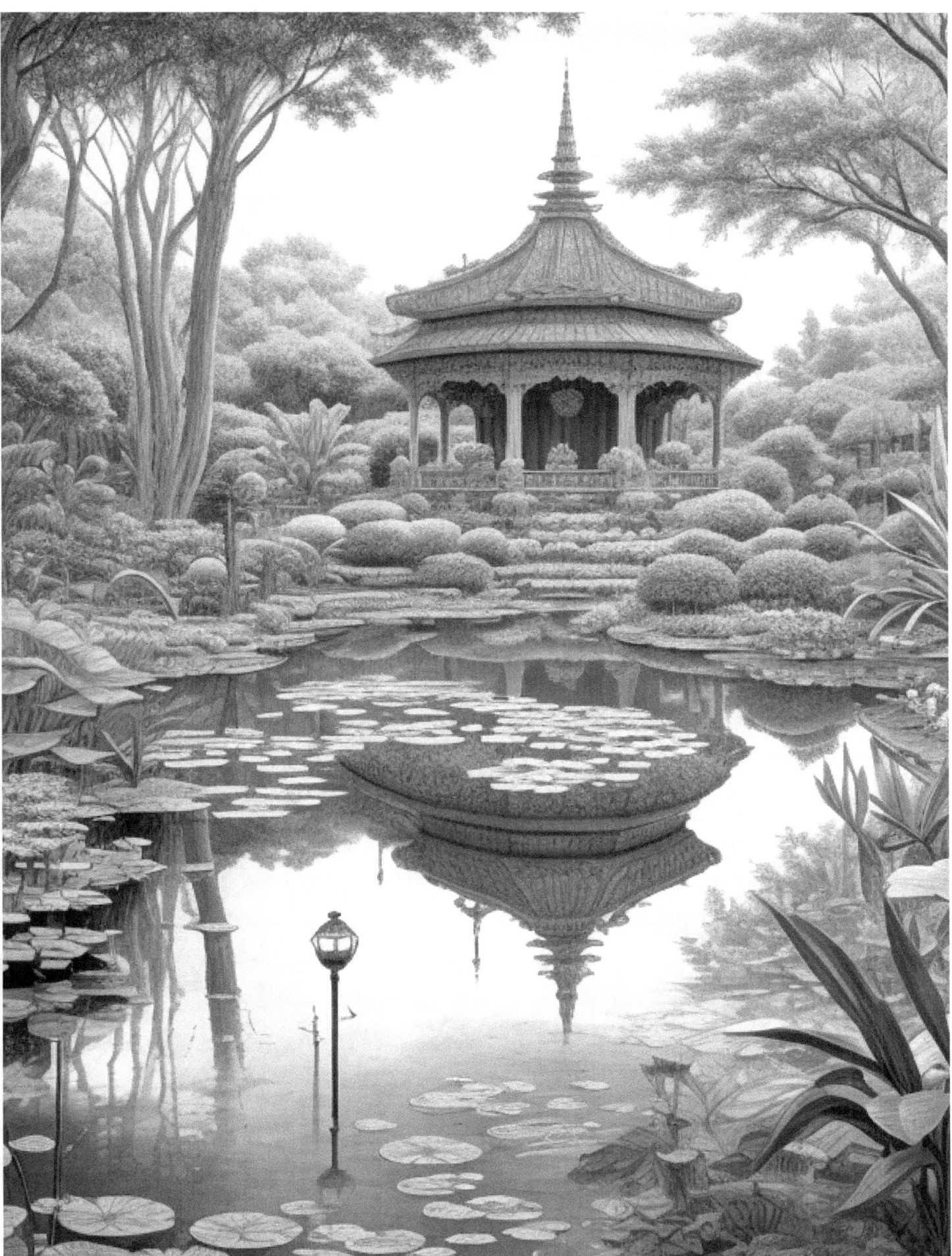

This Page is Intentionally Left Blank to Prevent Bleed Through.

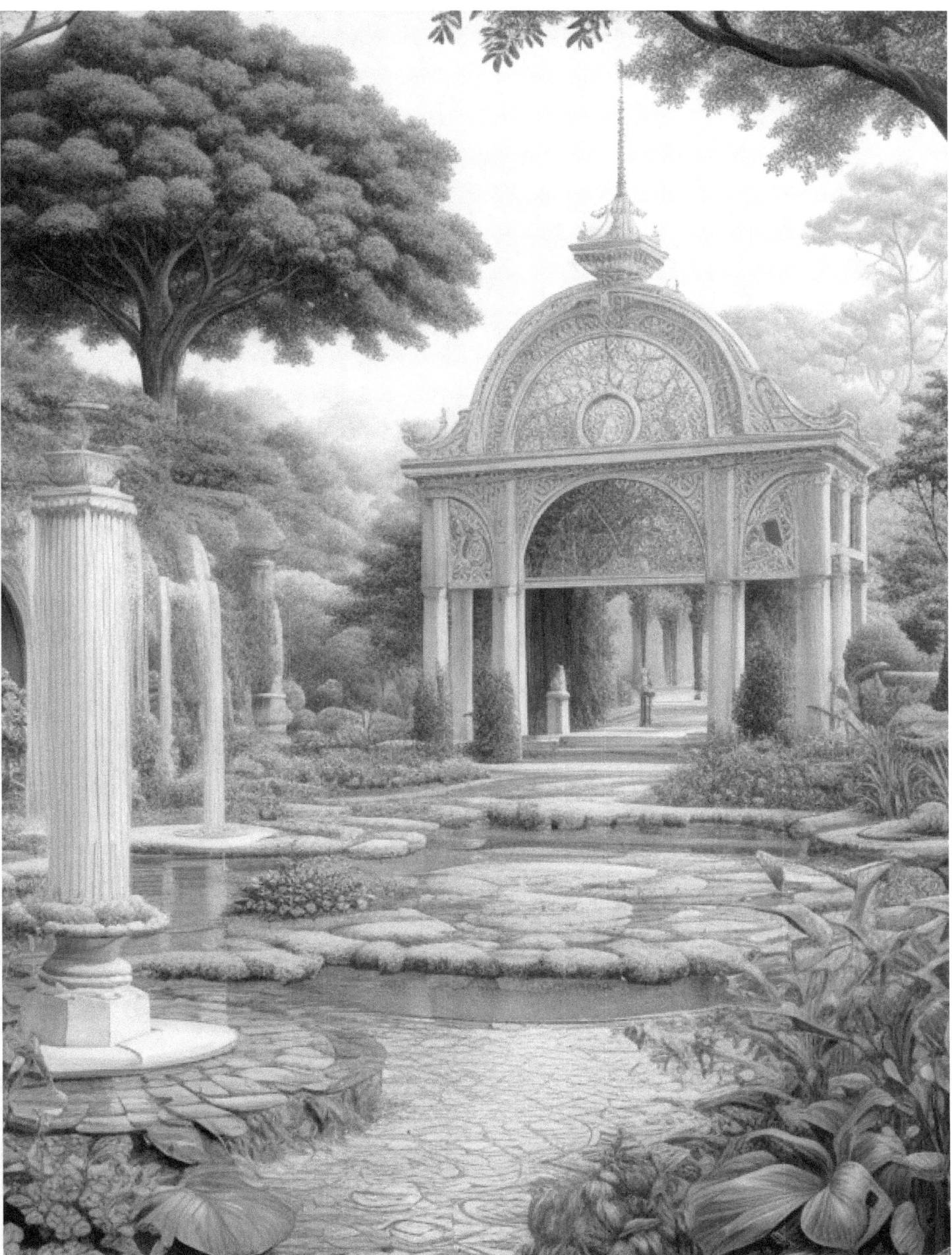

This Page is Intentionally Left Blank to Prevent Bleed Through.

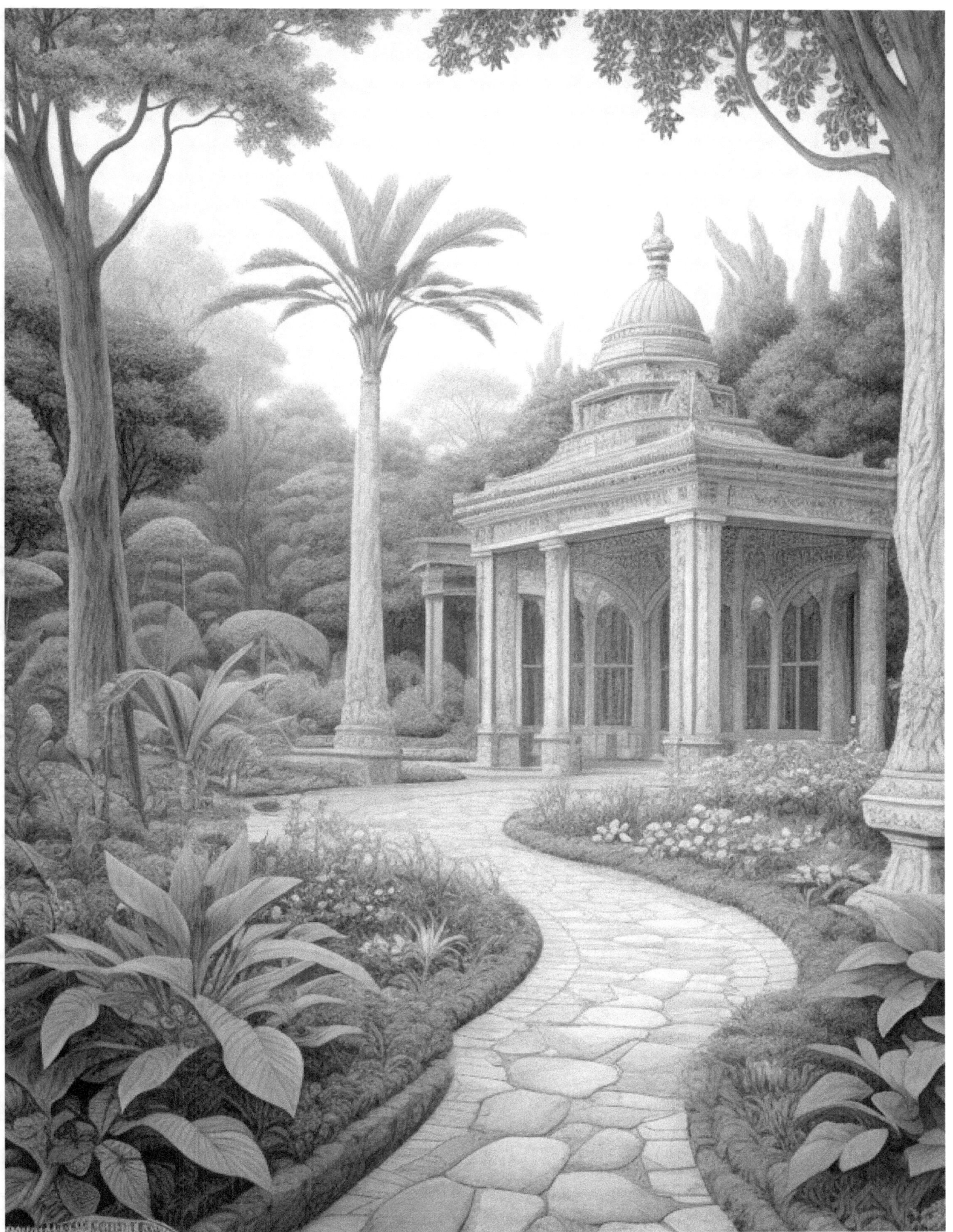

This Page is Intentionally Left Blank to Prevent Bleed Through.

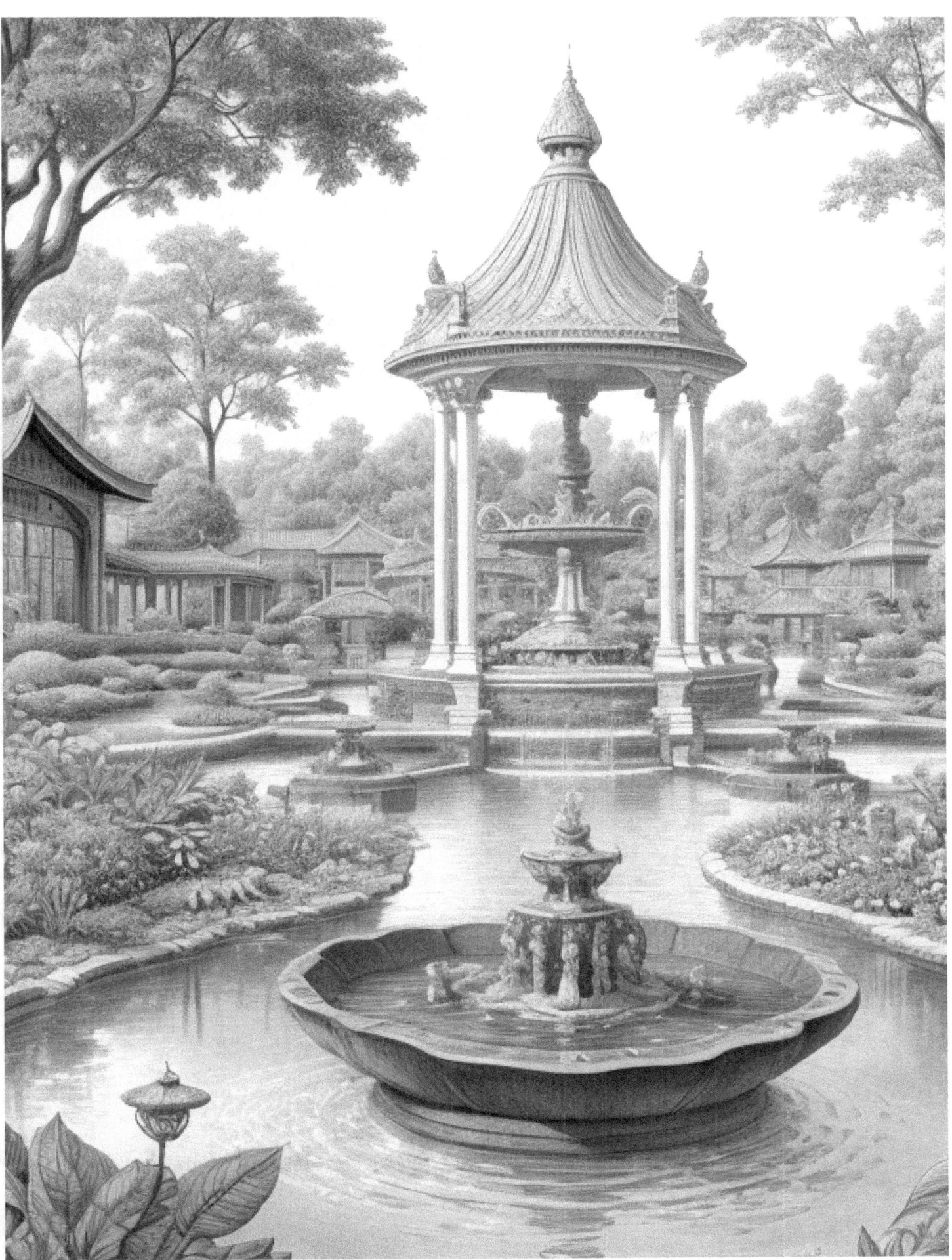

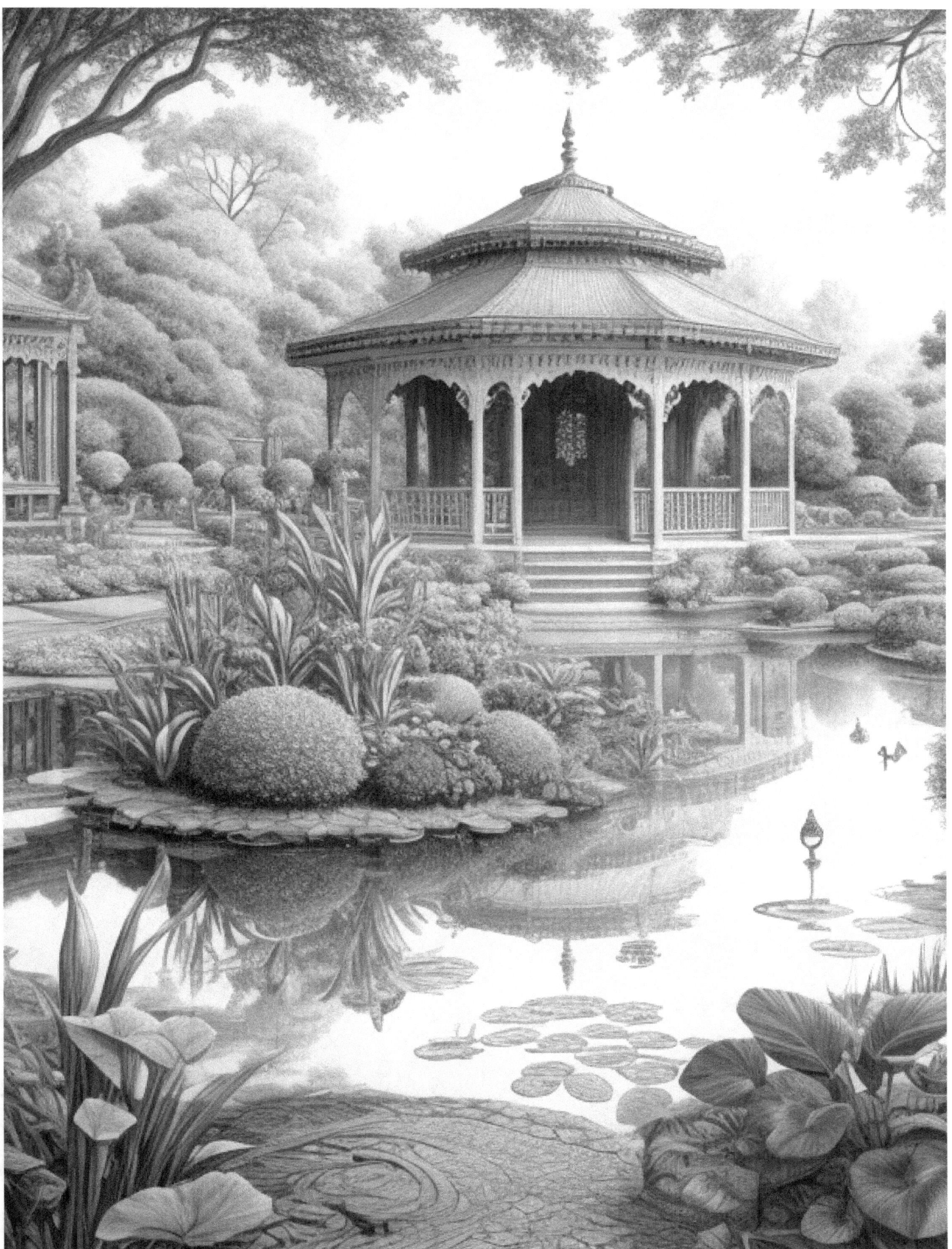

This Page is Intentionally Left Blank to Prevent Bleed Through.

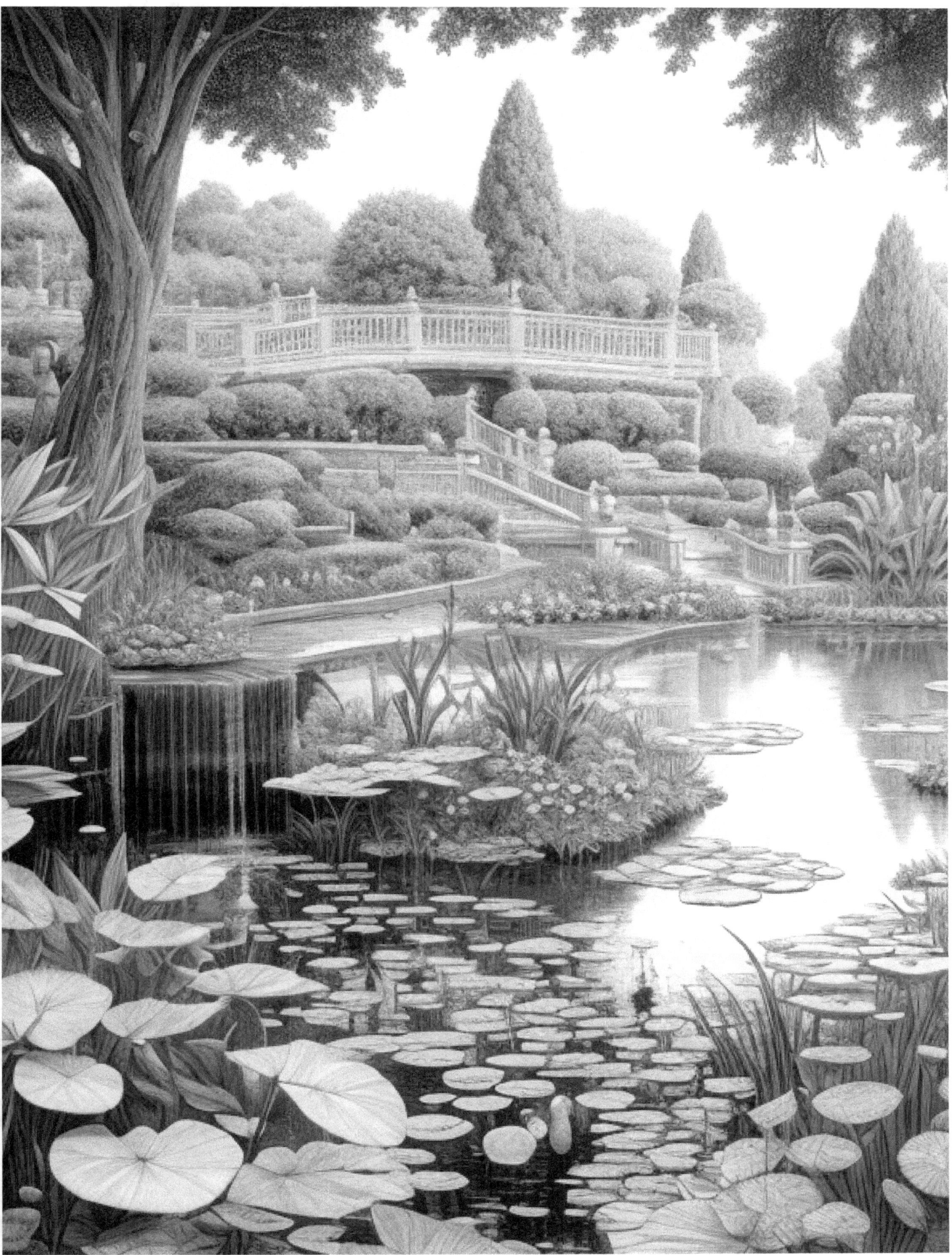

This Page is Intentionally Left Blank to Prevent Bleed Through.

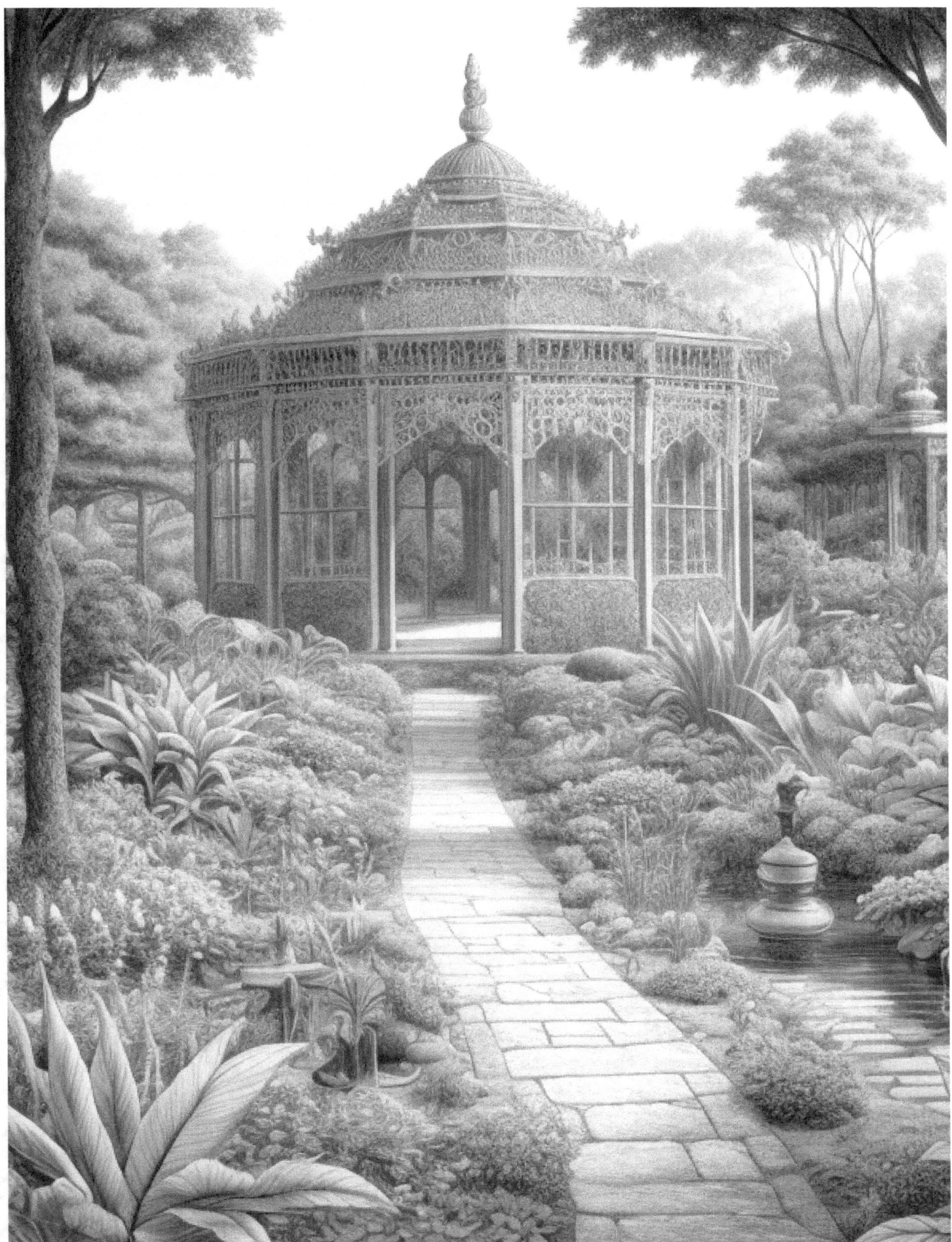

This Page is Intentionally Left Blank to Prevent Bleed Through.

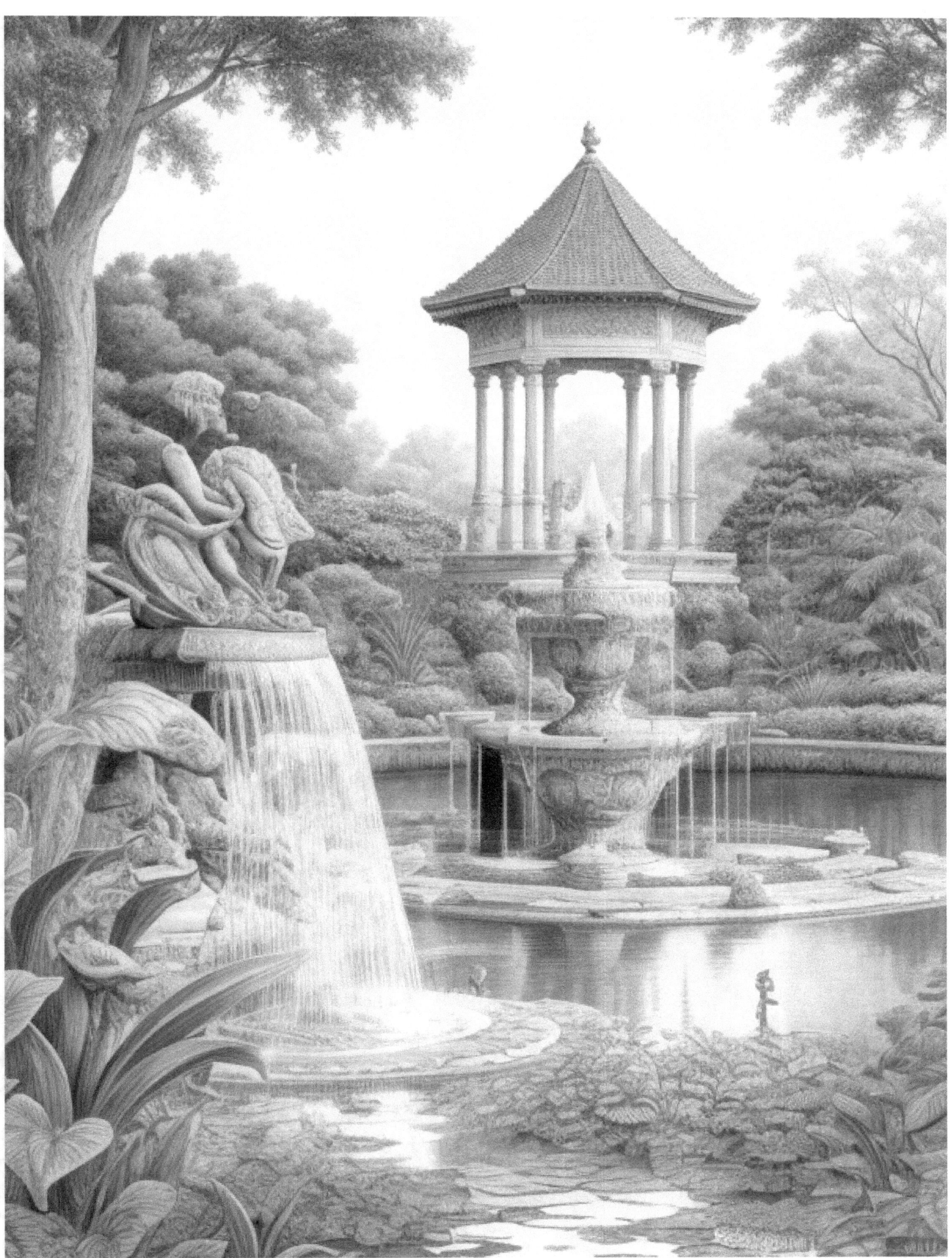

This Page is Intentionally Left Blank to Prevent Bleed Through.

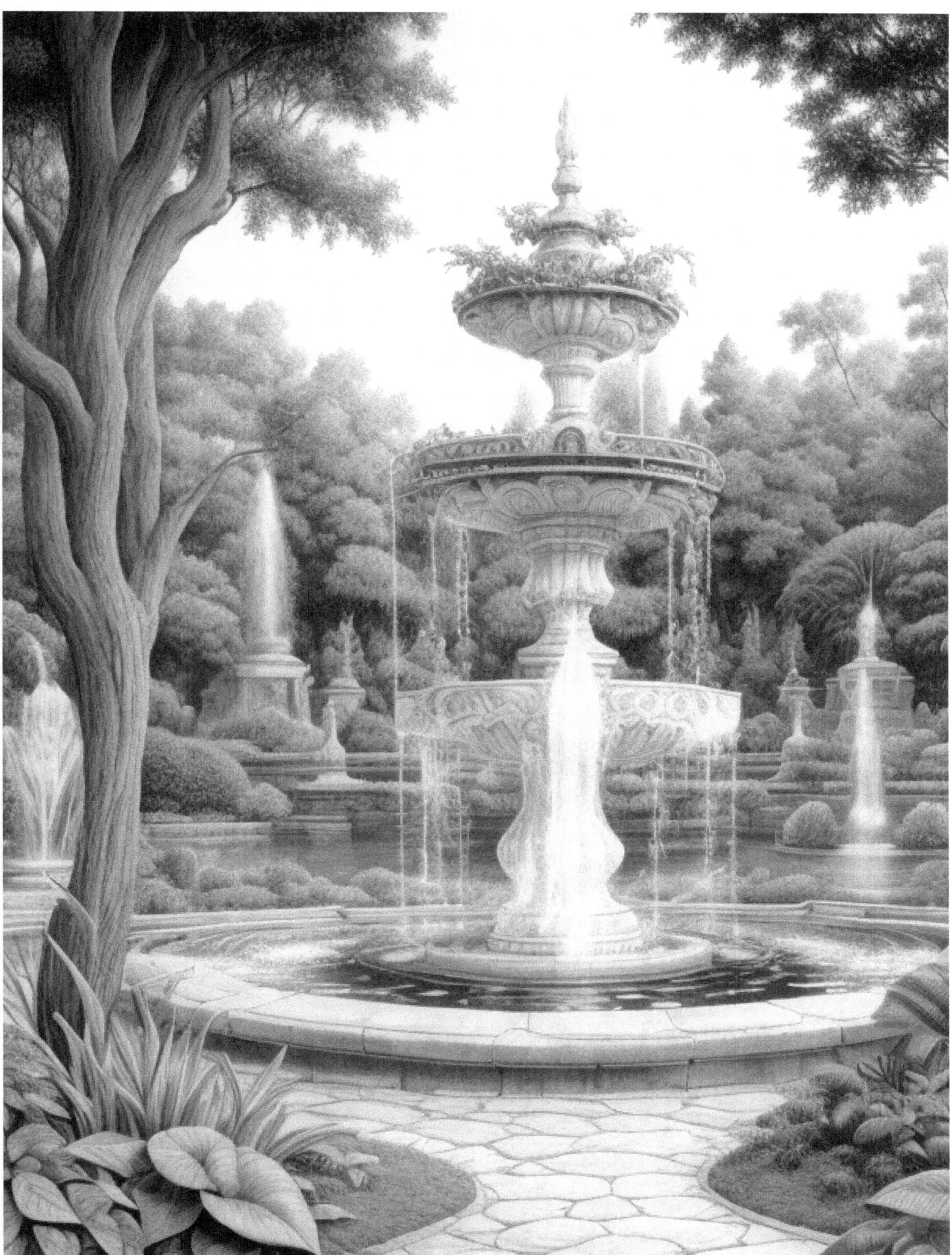

This Page is Intentionally Left Blank to Prevent Bleed Through.

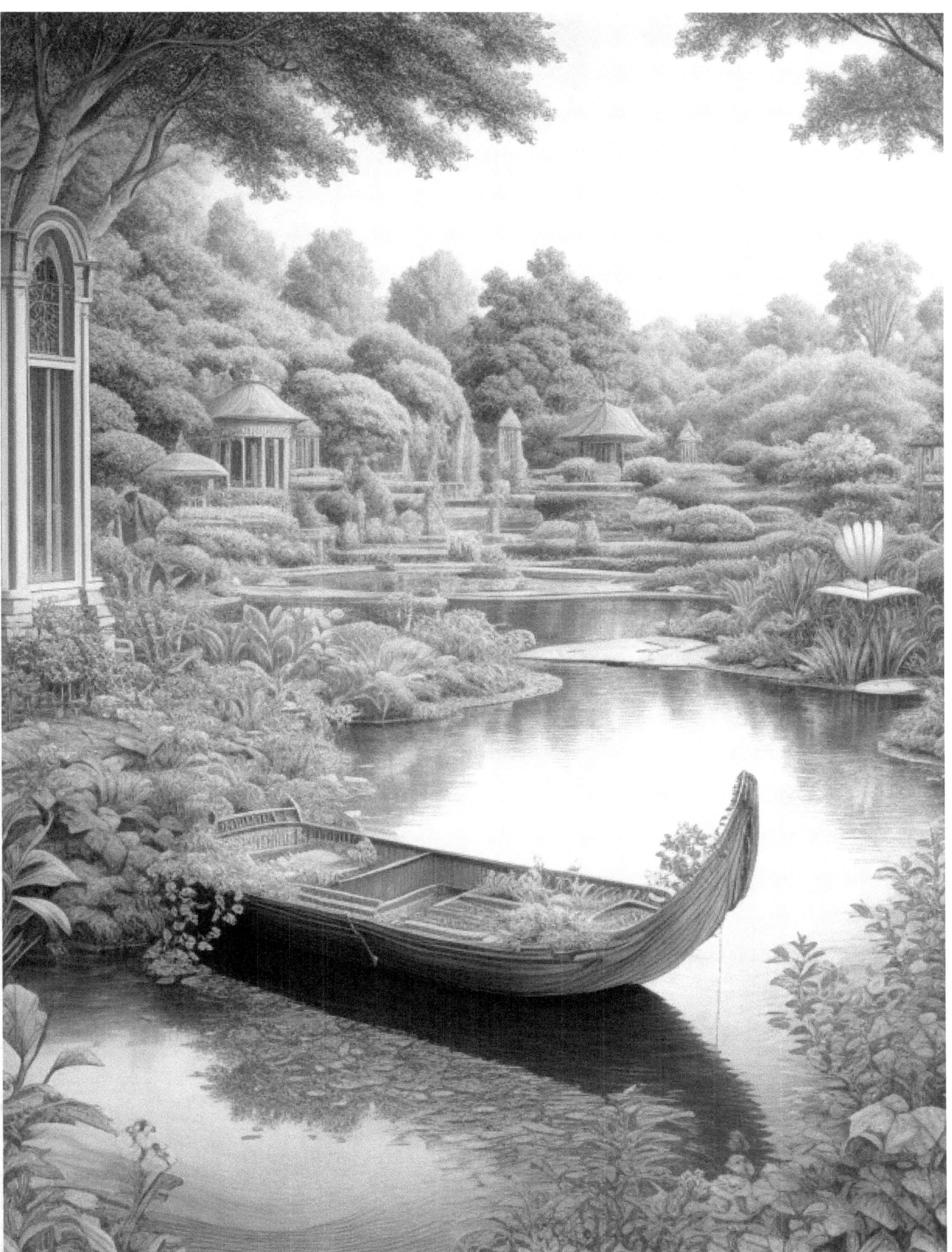

This Page is Intentionally Left Blank to Prevent Bleed Through.

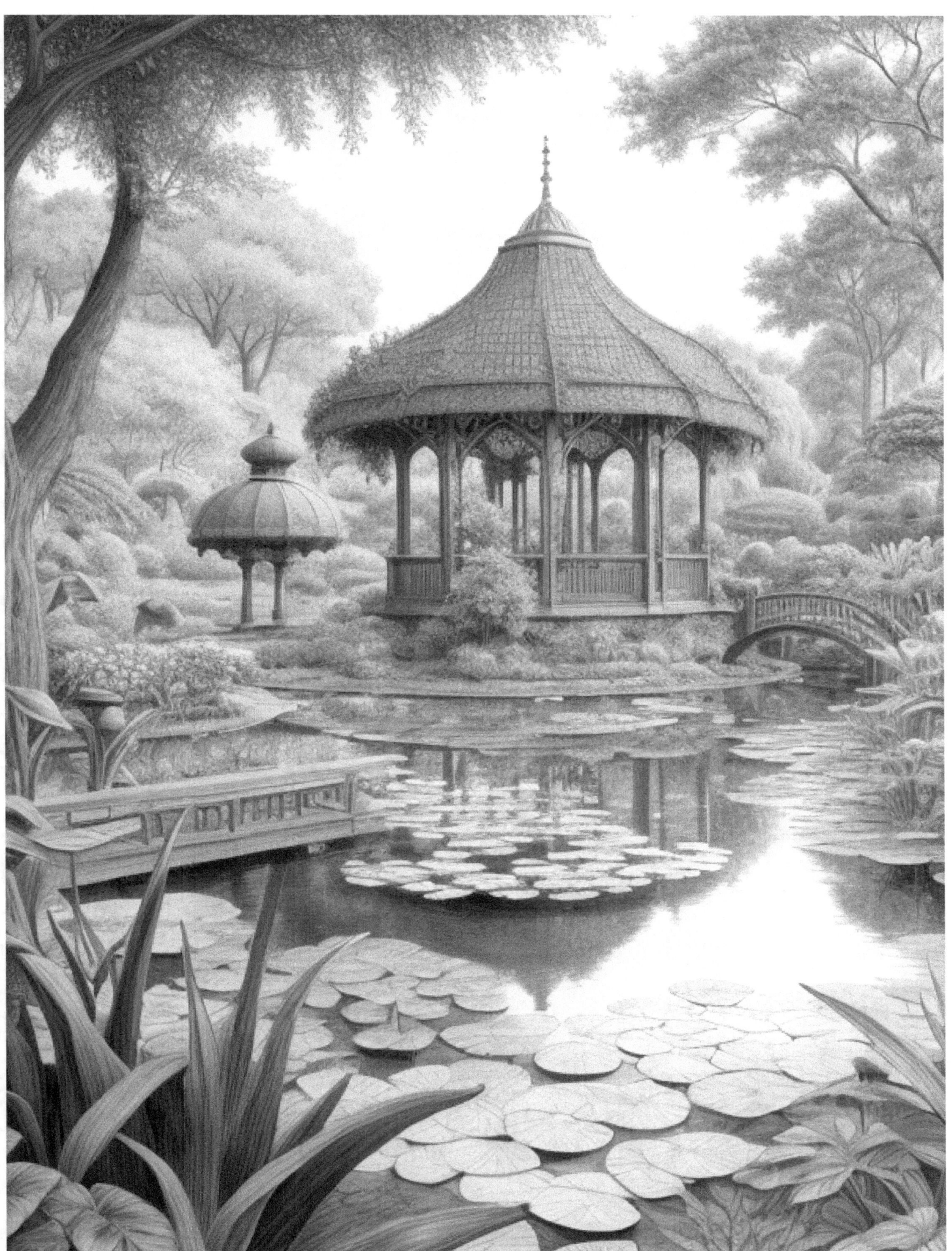

This Page is Intentionally Left Blank to Prevent Bleed Through.

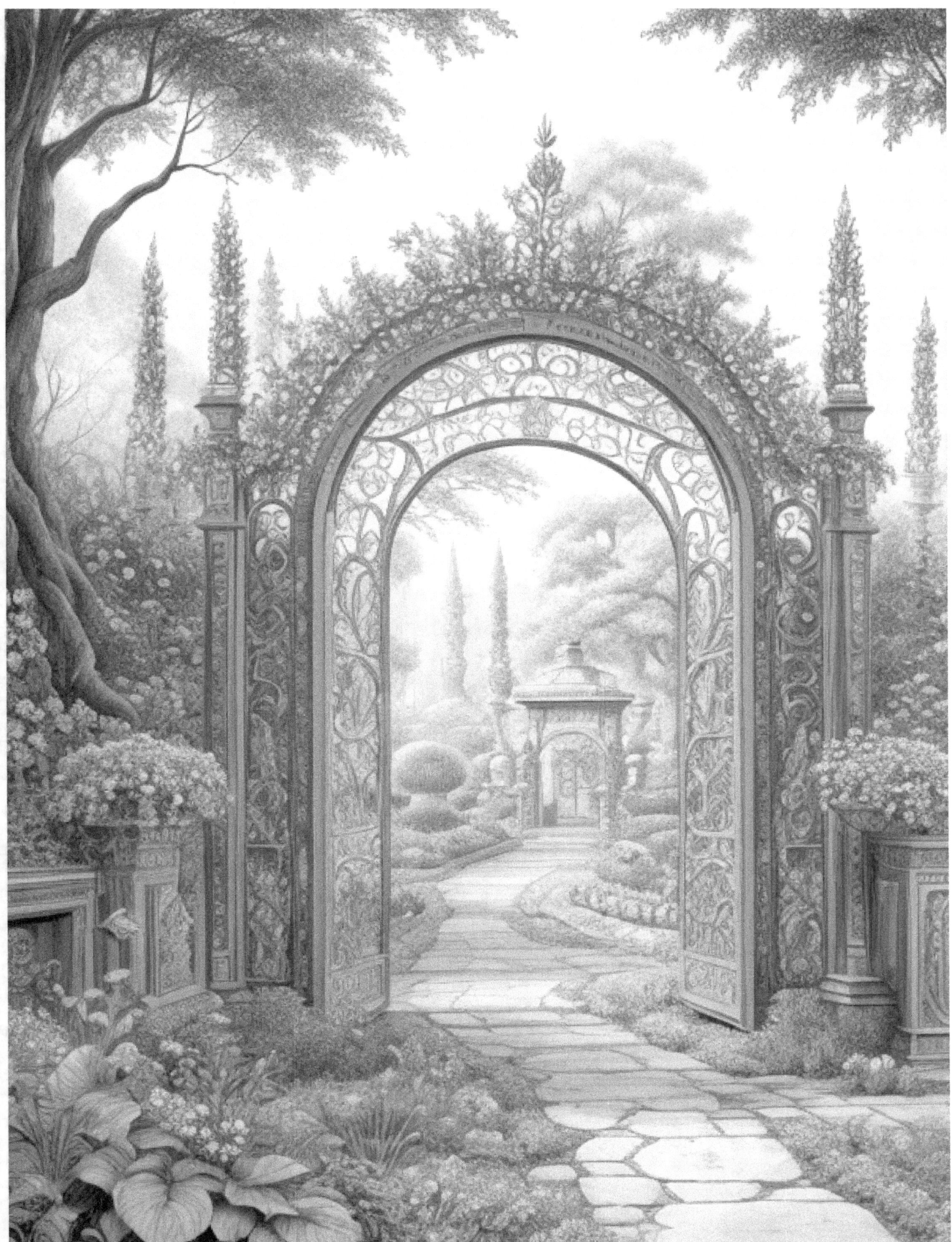

This Page is Intentionally Left Blank to Prevent Bleed Through.

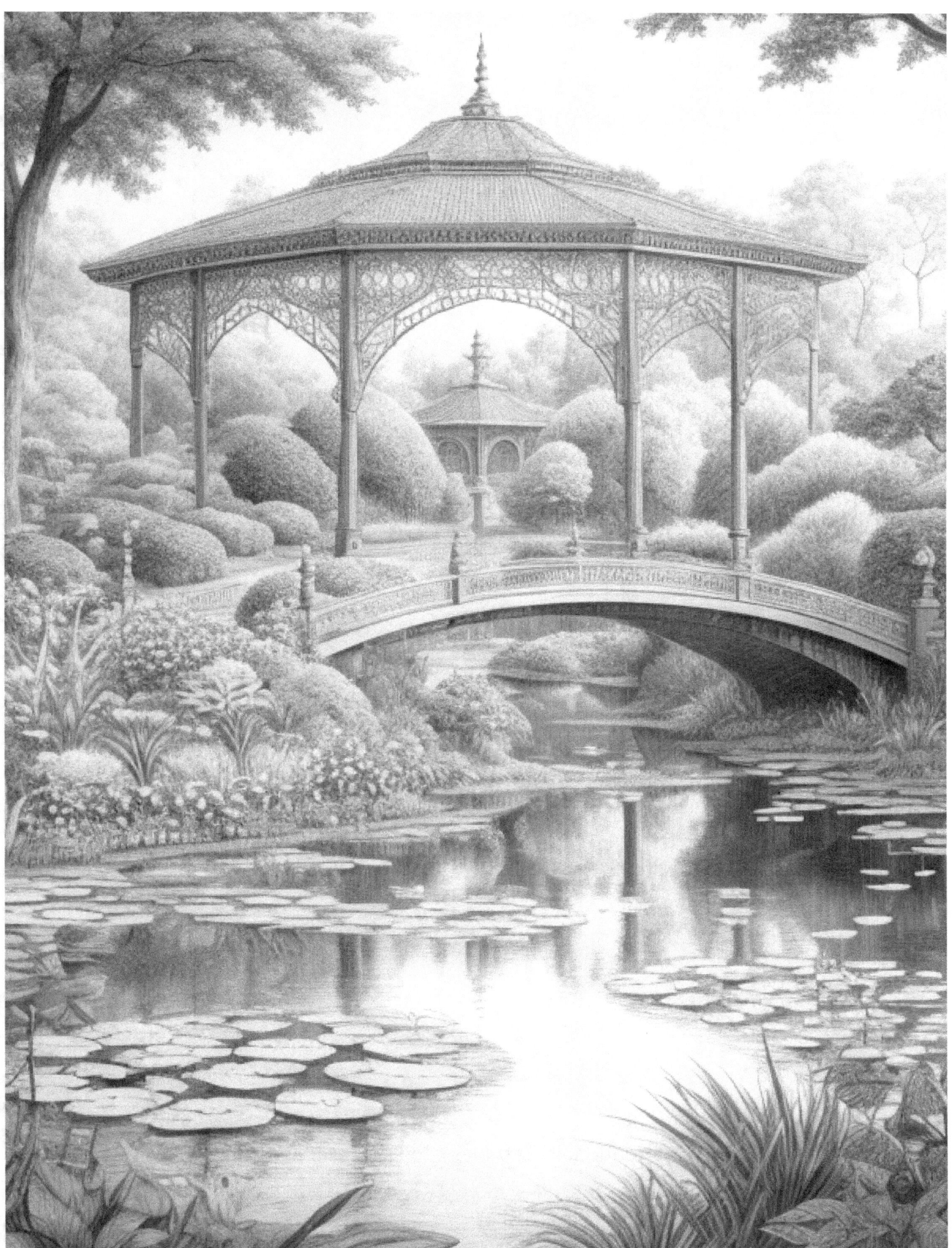

This Page is Intentionally Left Blank to Prevent Bleed Through.

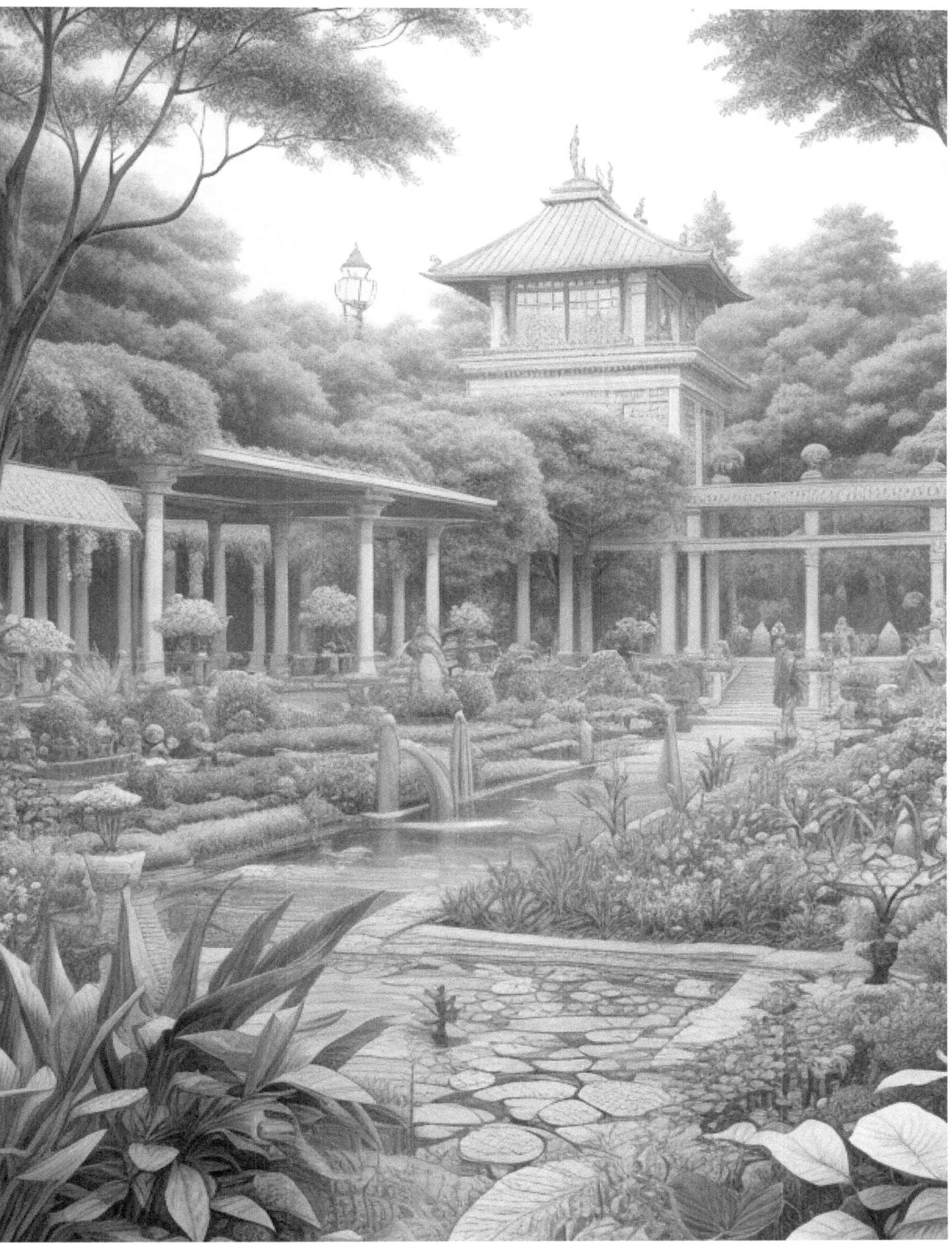

This Page is Intentionally Left Blank to Prevent Bleed Through.

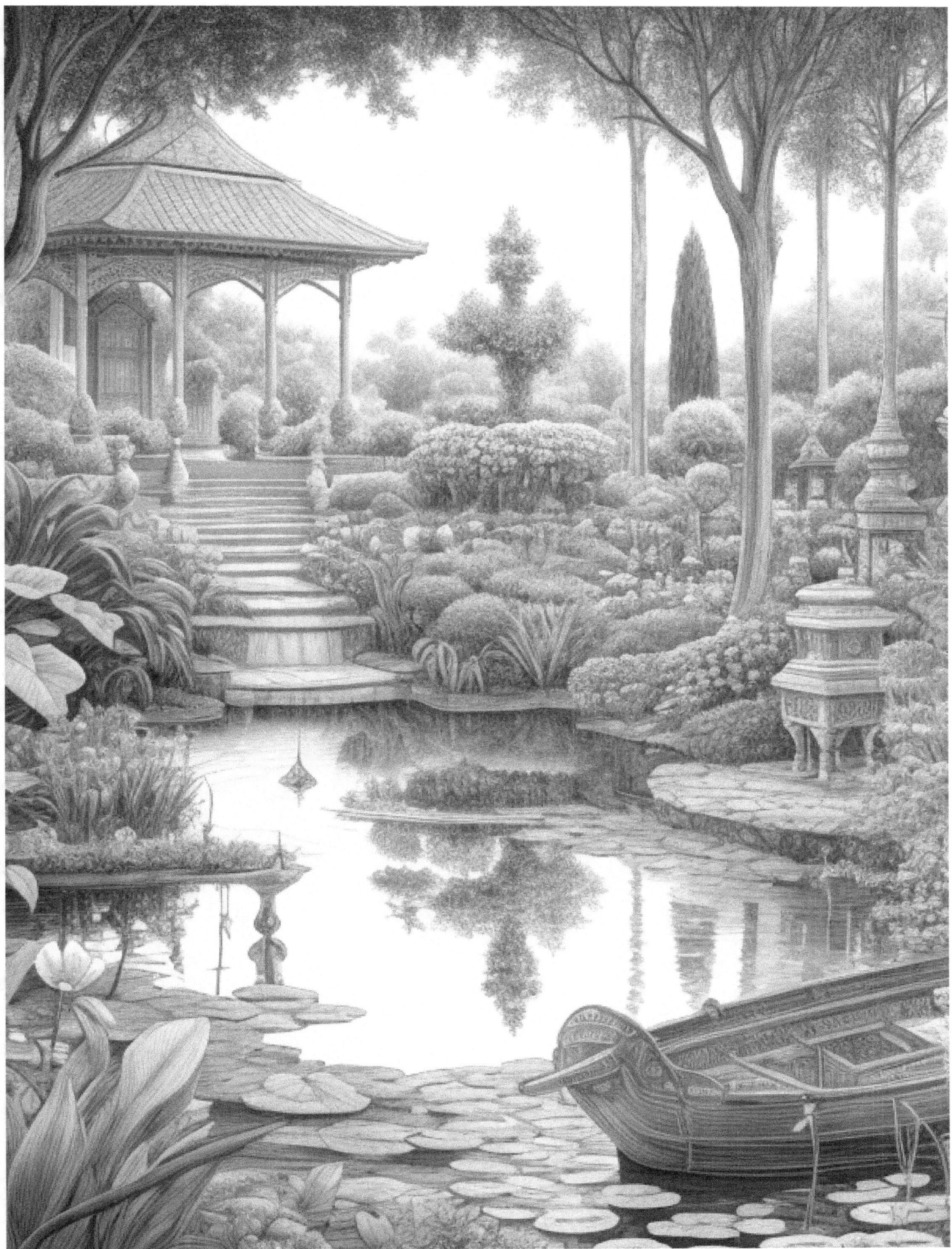

This Page is Intentionally Left Blank to Prevent Bleed Through.

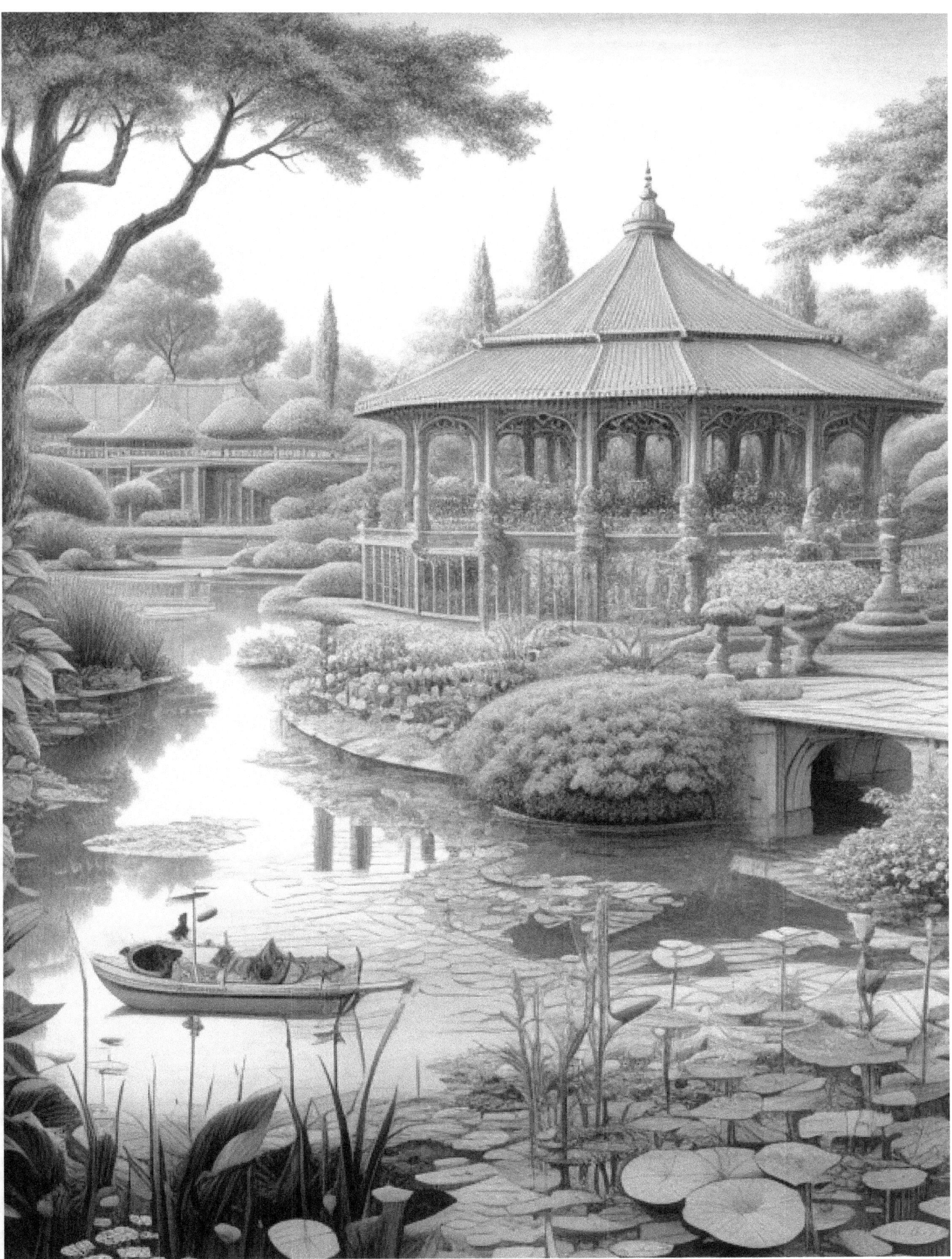

This Page is Intentionally Left Blank to Prevent Bleed Through.

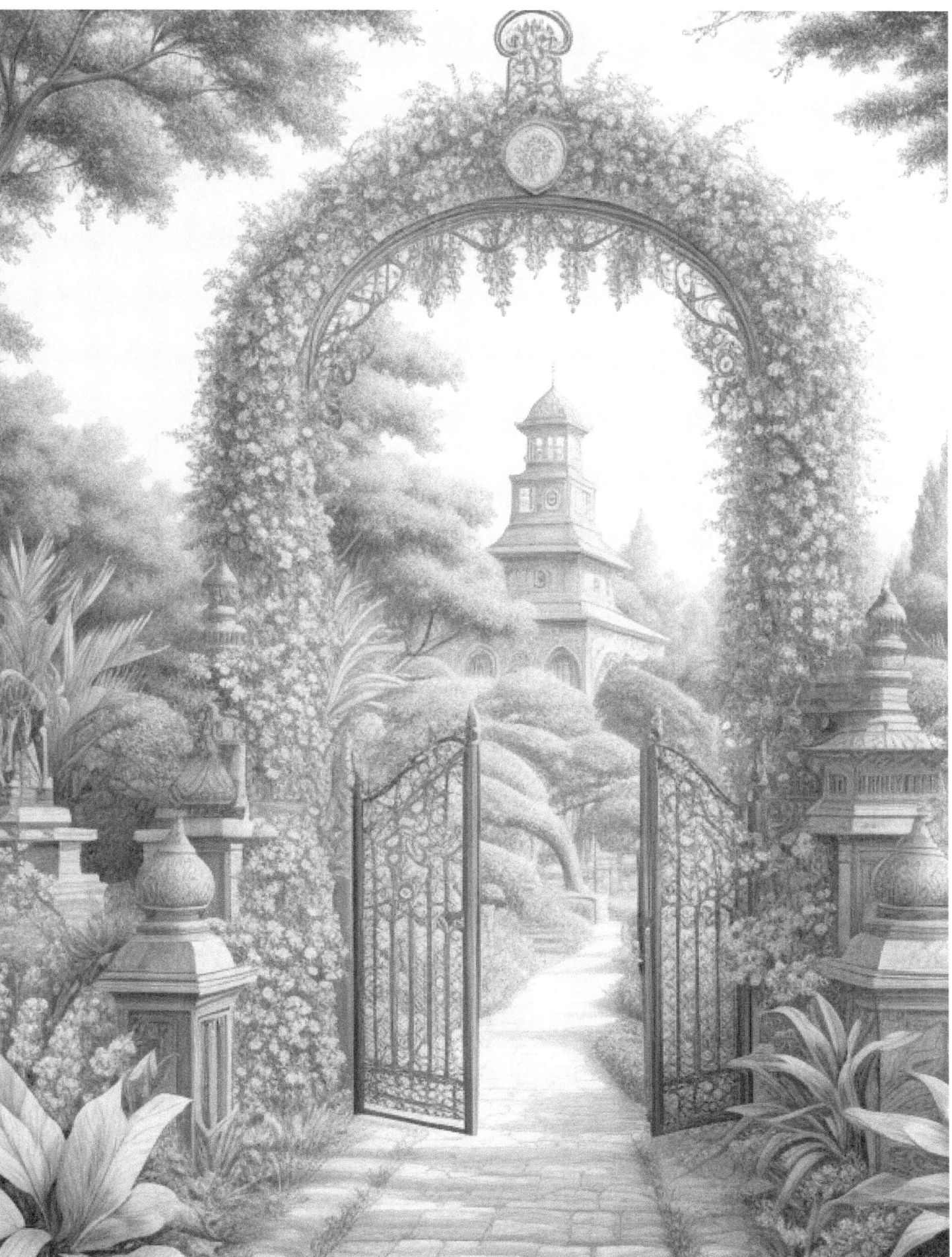

This Page is Intentionally Left Blank to Prevent Bleed Through.

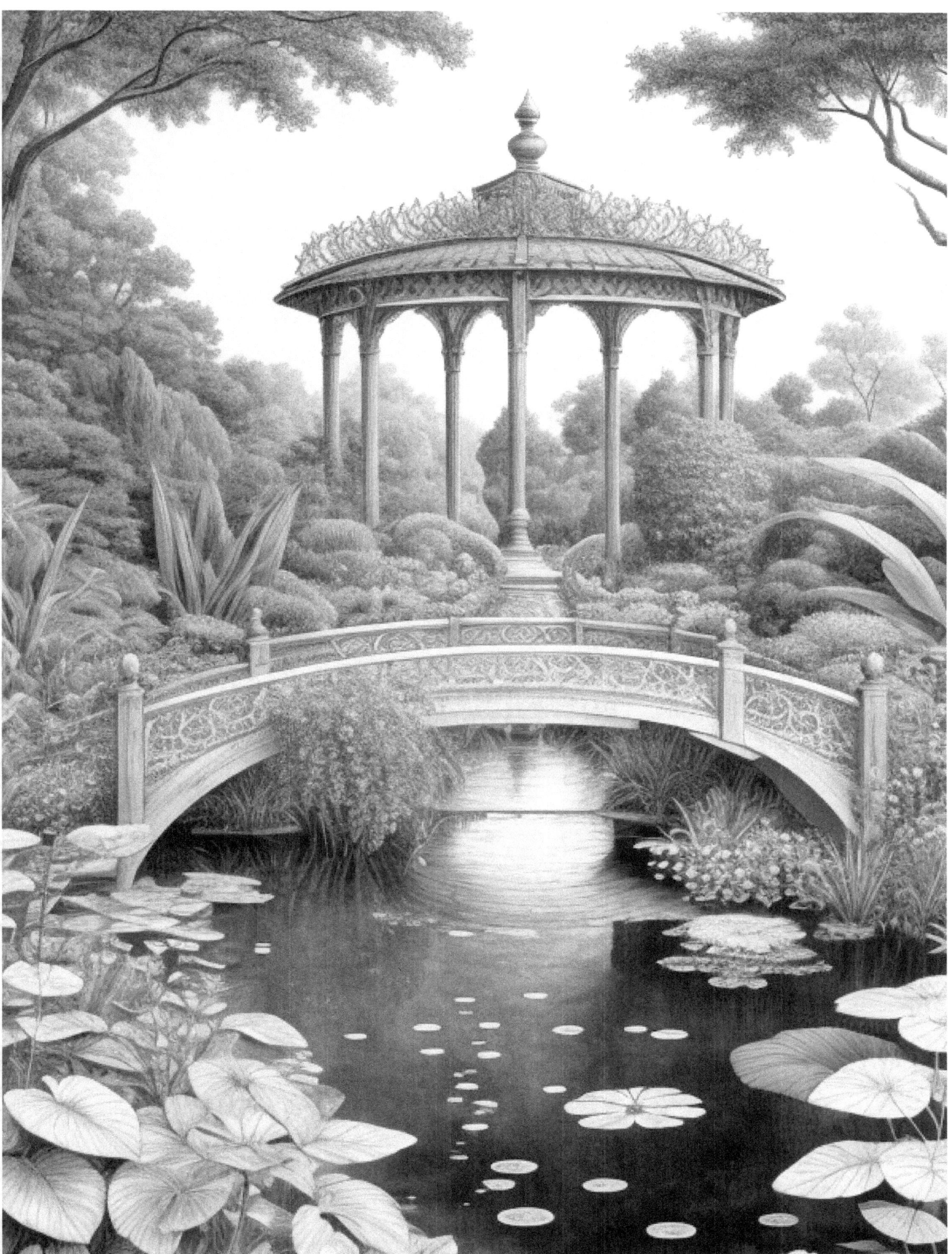

This Page is Intentionally Left Blank to Prevent Bleed Through.

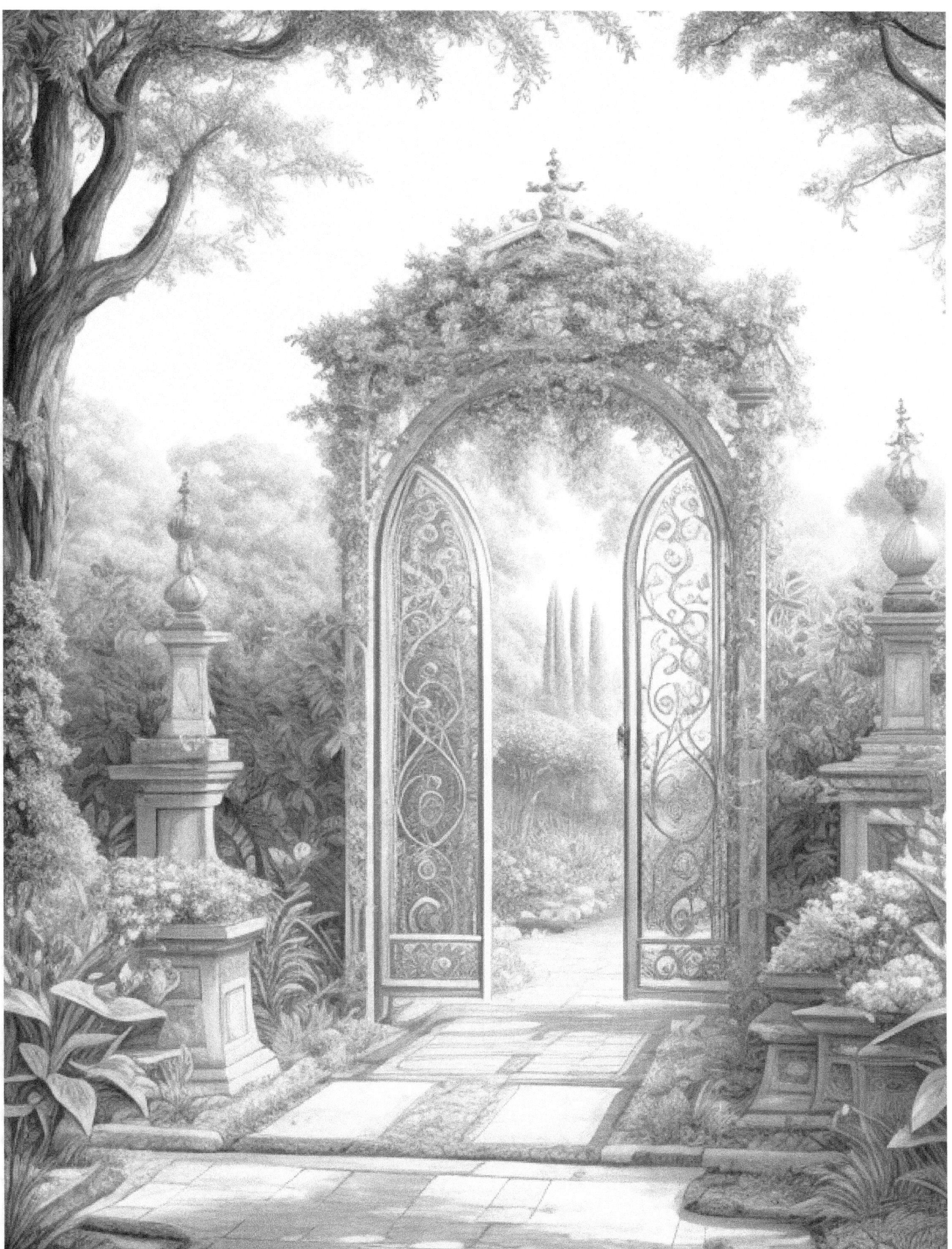

This Page is Intentionally Left Blank to Prevent Bleed Through.

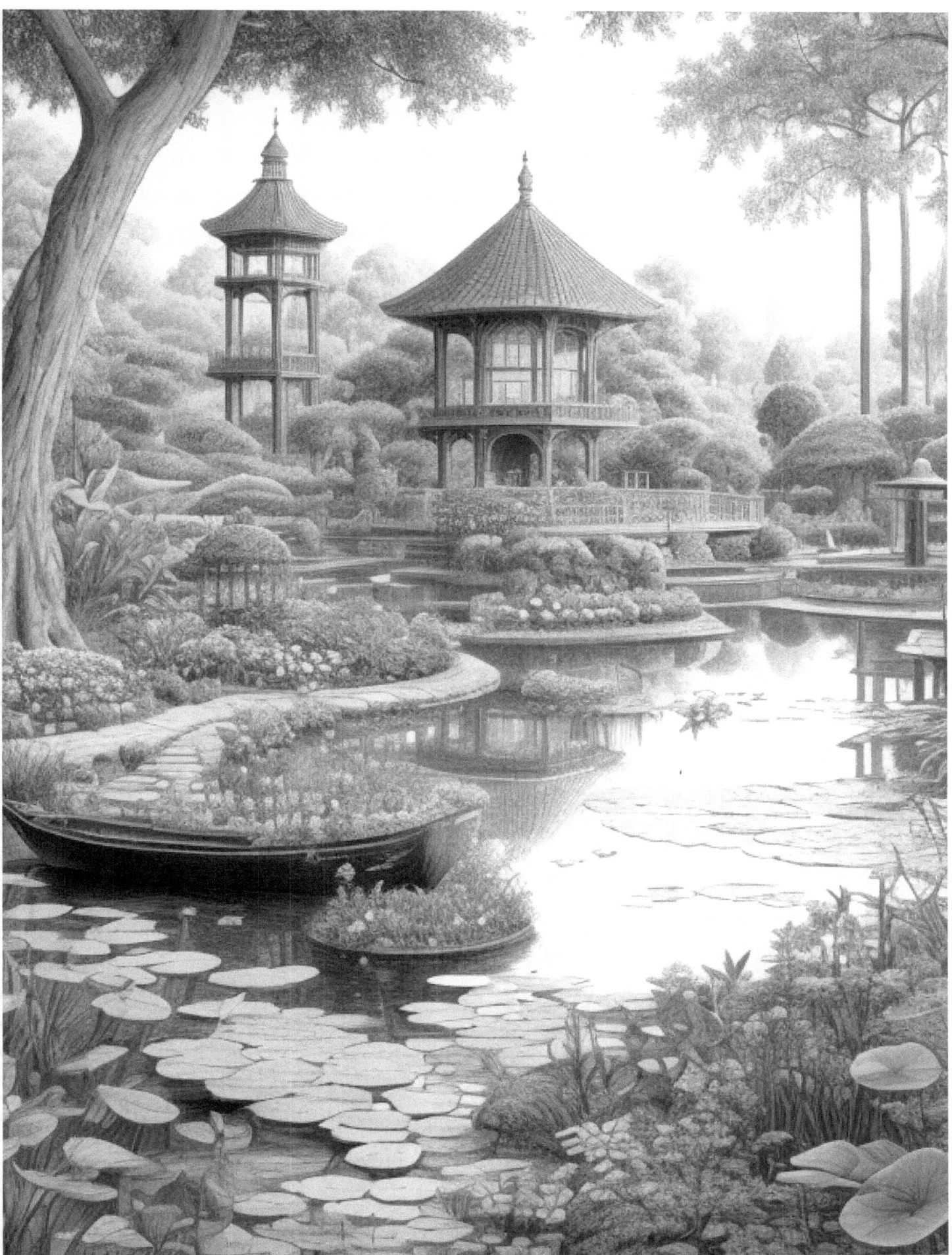

This Page is Intentionally Left Blank to Prevent Bleed Through.

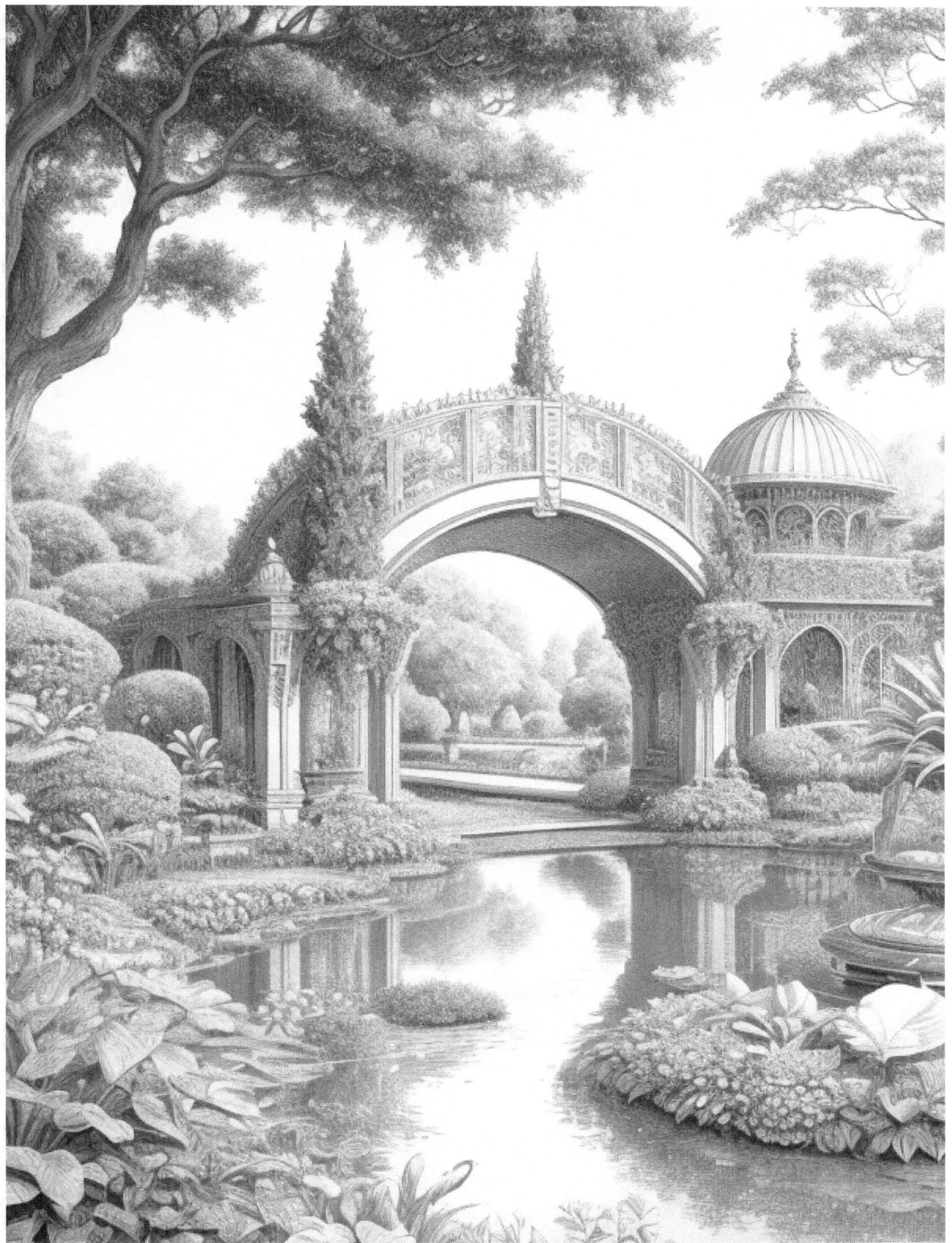

This Page is Intentionally Left Blank to Prevent Bleed Through.

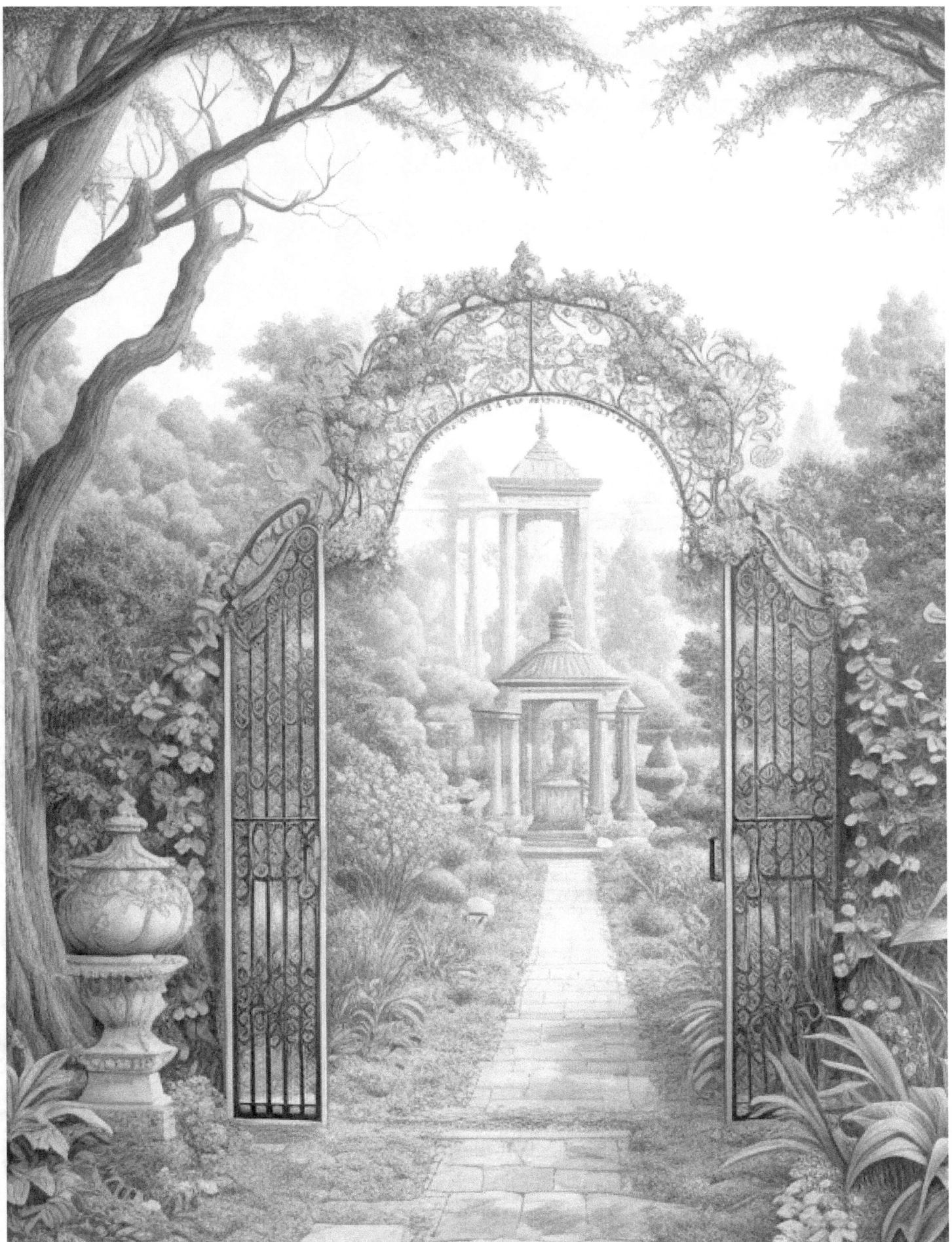

This Page is Intentionally Left Blank to Prevent Bleed Through.

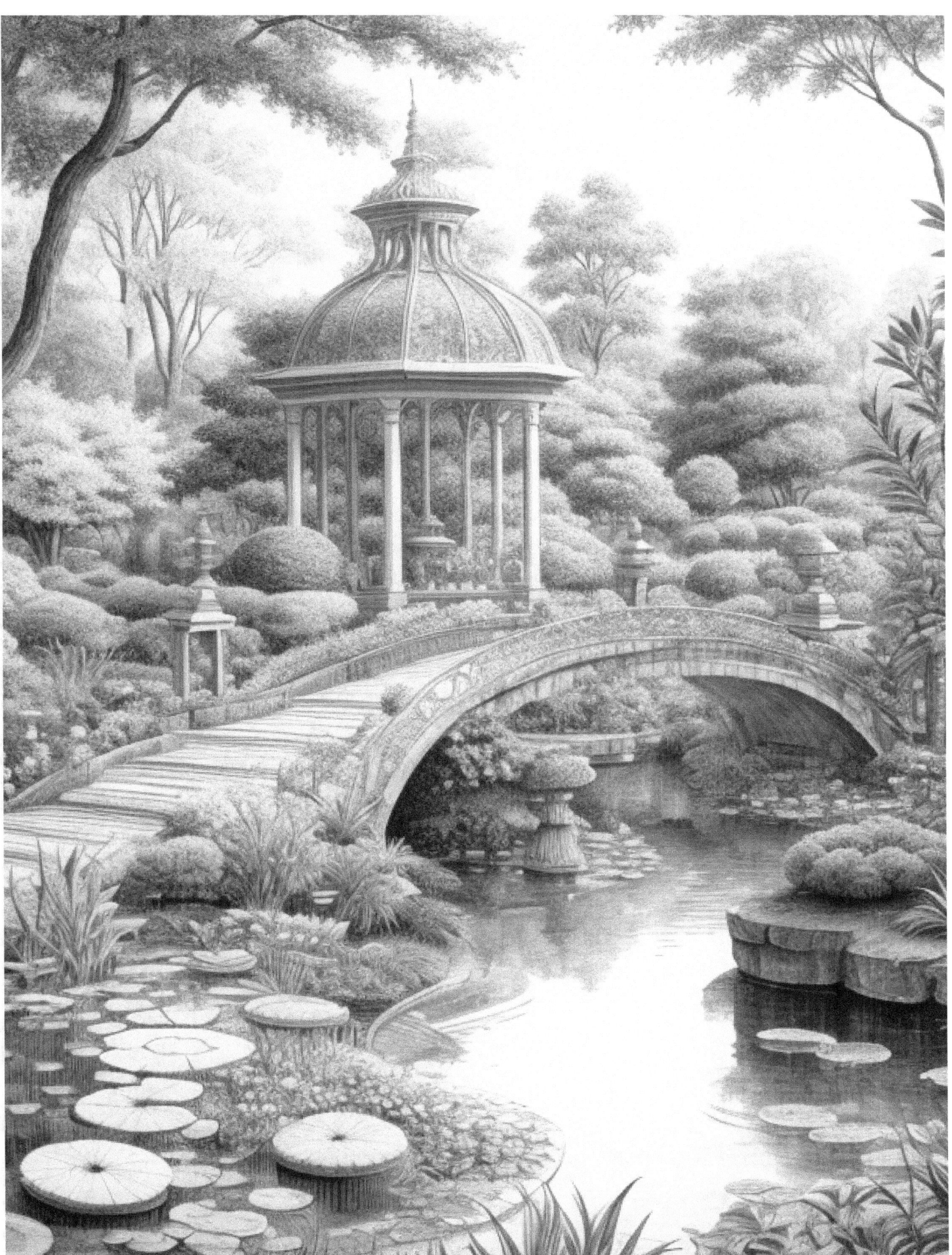

This Page is Intentionally Left Blank to Prevent Bleed Through.

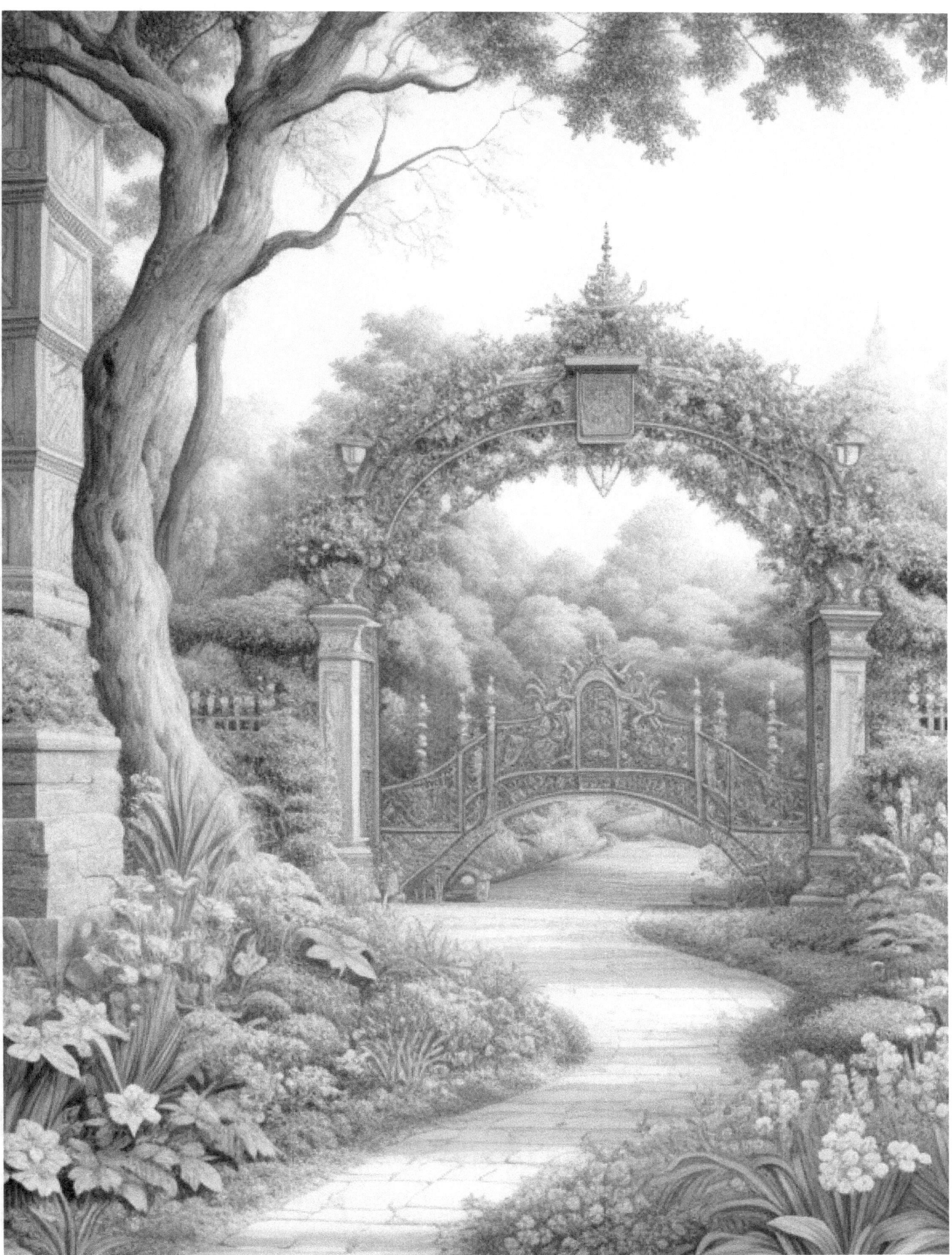

This Page is Intentionally Left Blank to Prevent Bleed Through.

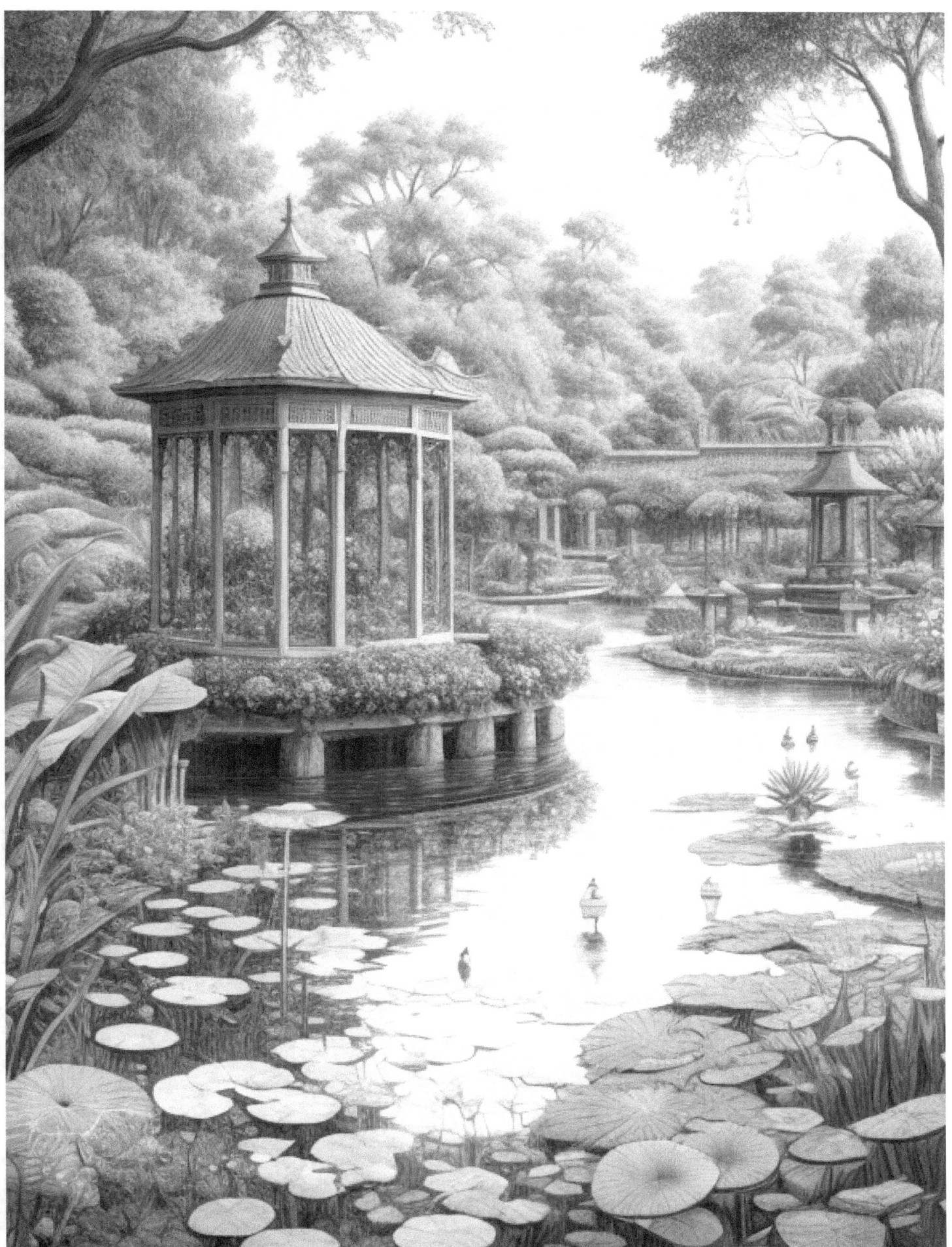

This Page is Intentionally Left Blank to Prevent Bleed Through.

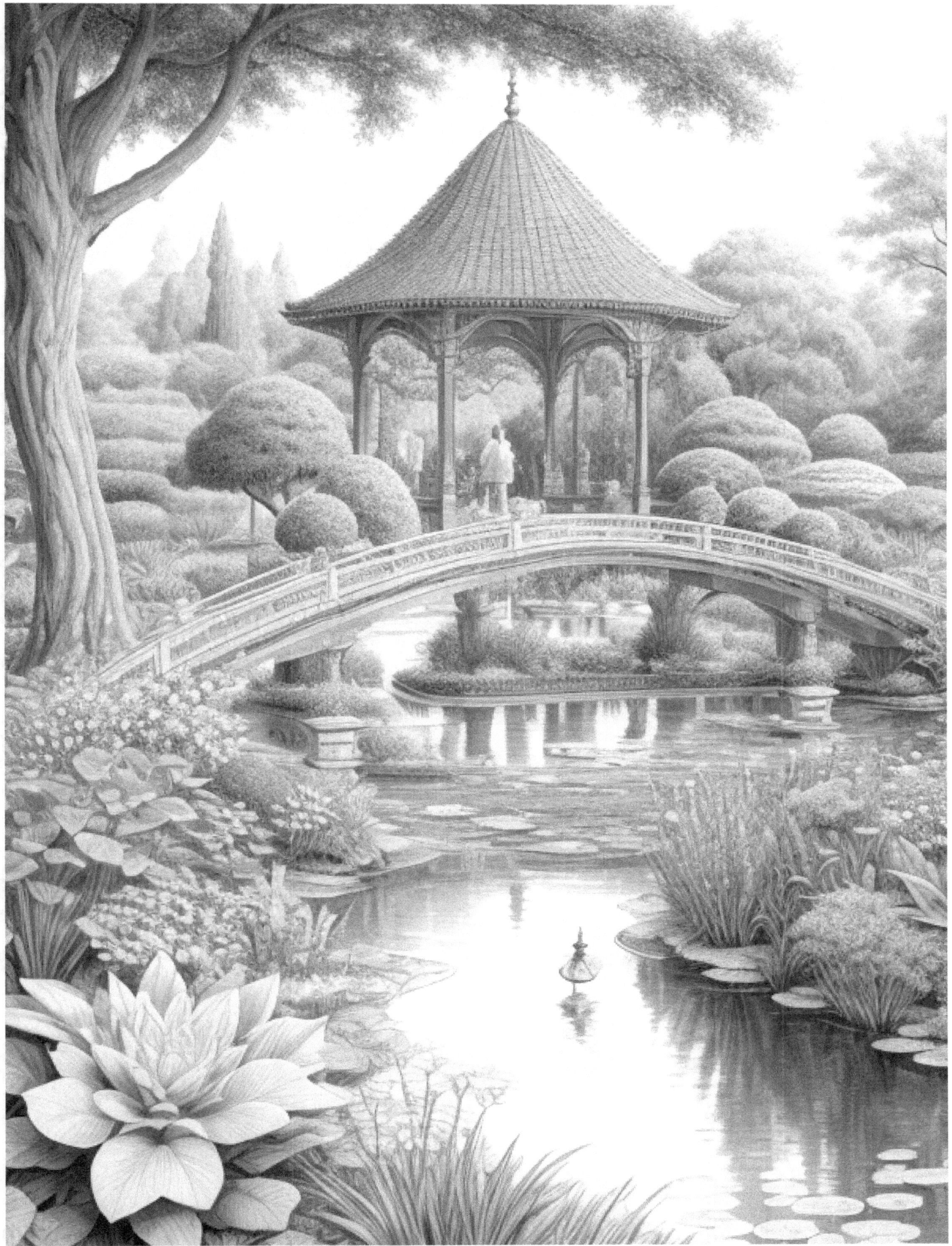

This Page is Intentionally Left Blank to Prevent Bleed Through.

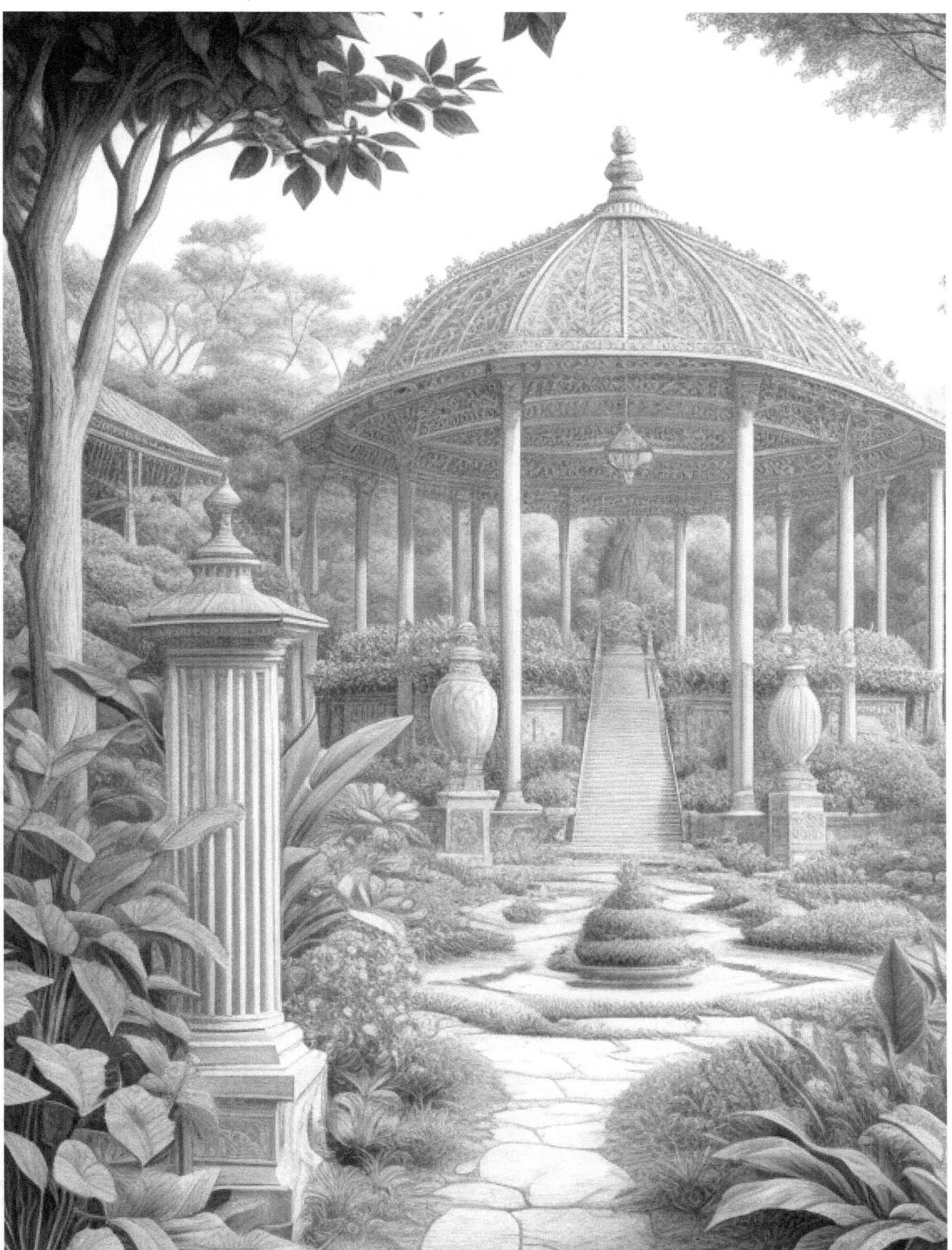

This Page is Intentionally Left Blank to Prevent Bleed Through.

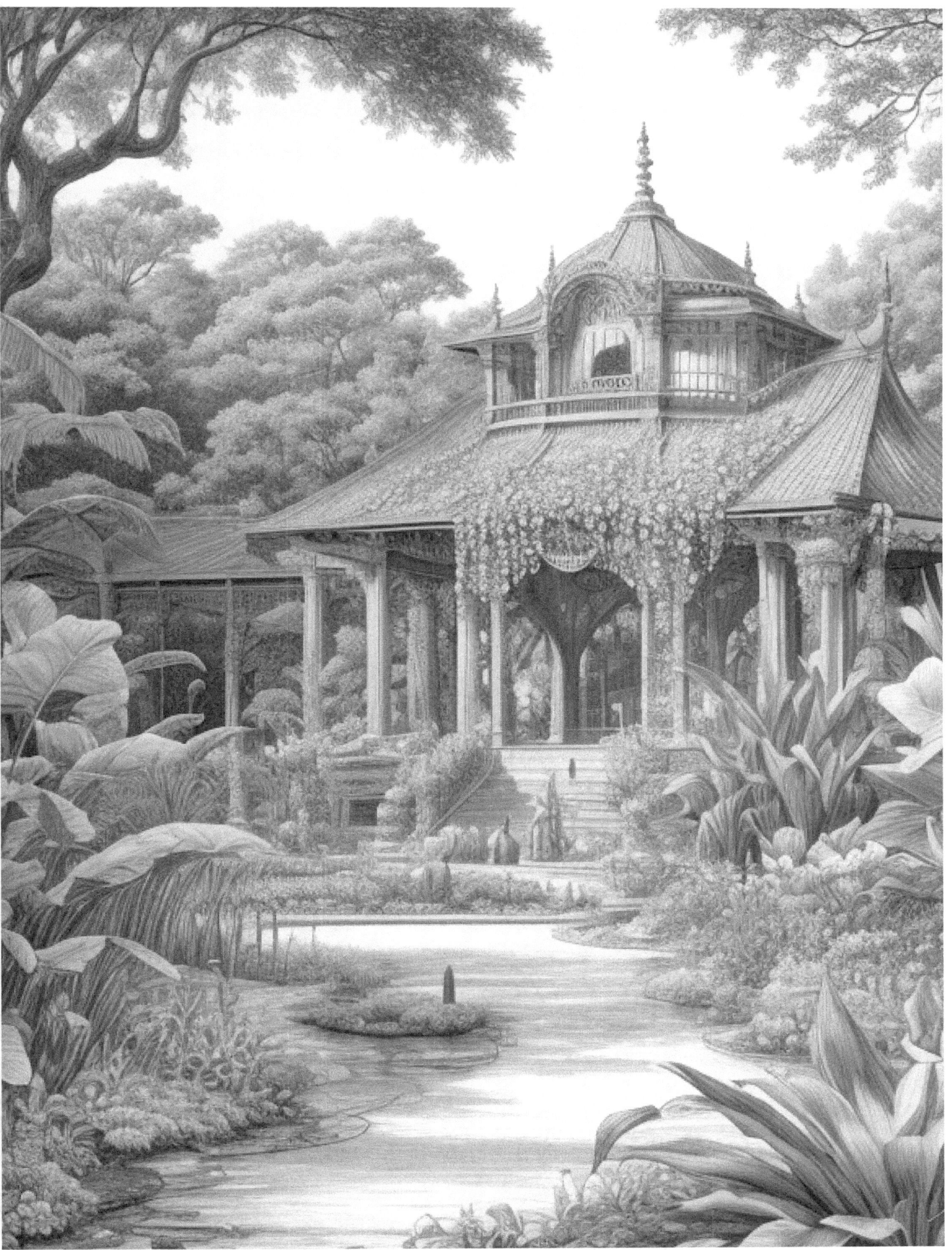

This Page is Intentionally Left Blank to Prevent Bleed Through.

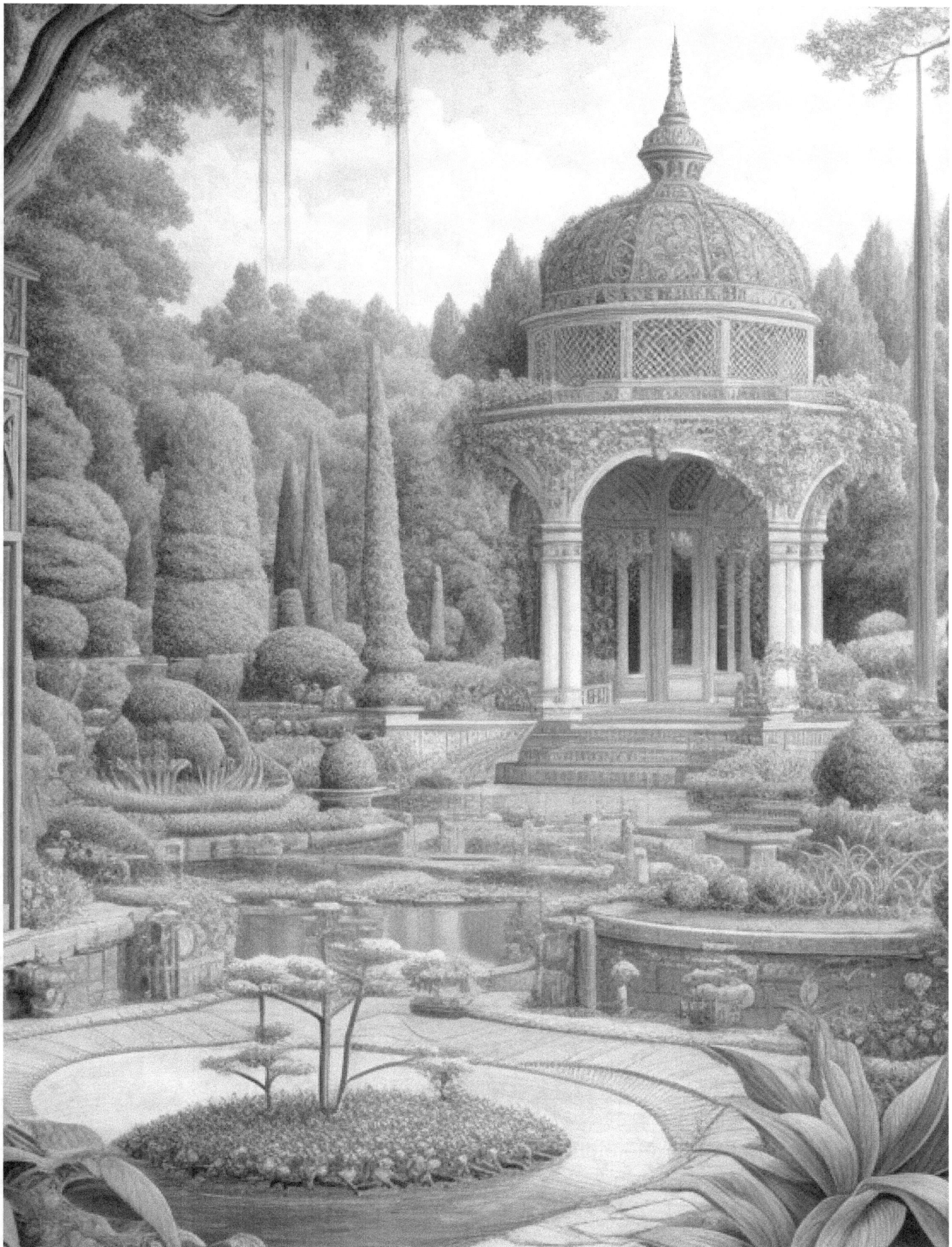